JOHN GALSWORTHY

BY

HERMON OULD

CHAPMAN & HALL LTD
LONDON

First published
1934
CHAPMAN & HALL LTD
11 *Henrietta Street*
LONDON
W.C.2

MADE AND PRINTED IN GREAT BRITAIN BY
EBENEZER BAYLIS AND SON, LIMITED, THE
TRINITY PRESS, WORCESTER, AND LONDON.
Bound by G. and J. Kitcat, Limited, London.

Glasgow University Library

Sarah Davies.

JOHN GALSWORTHY

Photo: *Arche M. Dunning.*

JOHN GALSWORTHY
California, Winter 1925.

Frontispiece.

CONTENTS

CONTENTS

ILLUSTRATIONS

ACKNOWLEDGMENTS

MY THANKS to Mrs. Galsworthy for the loan of the pictures facing pages, 22, 108, 228, and the frontispiece, and for many other things less easily estimated; to Mr. R. H. Sauter for the medallion on the cover; to Mr. H. Dennis Bradley for permission to quote the letters on pages 234 and 235; to Mr. Leon M. Lion for pictures of scenes from *The Skin Game* and *Justice*; to Miss Irene Rooke and Mr. Milton Rosmer for photographs of characters from *The Fugitive*, *The Mob* and *The Silver Box*; to Madame Albanesi for the loan of the photograph of Meggie taken just before her death and given to her father; to Madame Jo van Ammers-Küller for the photograph facing page 46, to Monsieur Louis Piérard for that facing page 88, and to Herr Felix Salten for that facing page 96.

H. O.

FOREWORD

ALL portraits are partial. No man knows the whole truth even about himself, much less about another. A famous French critic, M. André Chevrillon, has said that no great English novelist of our times has shown so little of himself in his books as John Galsworthy; and yet I feel that the man Galsworthy as I knew him is perfectly revealed by his books. I never met a man or a woman who claimed to have been on terms of intimacy with Galsworthy—he was notoriously difficult to know; and yet I feel that I knew him. Neither do I claim to have been intimate with him, and yet the contact between us was so close that I do not remember ever to have been surprised by anything he said or did. There seems to have been a subtle understanding which had no need of words, and although during the ten years or so that I knew him we exchanged numerous letters, only the barest of references were ever made to the affectional basis of the relationship.

During the next decade many attempts will no doubt be made to estimate the significance of John Galsworthy. He figured prominently in so many worlds—the worlds of literature, the theatre, social service, international affairs—that studies from many angles will be required to produce a just picture of the complete man. The pages which follow are an attempt to give a purely personal appreciation, to record some of the details which went to the building-up of Galsworthy as he exists in my mind. How much the picture I give will be derived from personal contact with him over half a score of years, and how much to familiarity with his work spread over a much longer period, it is impossible to say. All I claim is that the picture is *my* picture; that I have not gleaned impressions and facts here and there among Galsworthy's friends and acquaintances, nor derived my opinion of his work from the usual critical sources. Indeed, very few pages of a critical nature will be found here; they are practically confined to a short chapter touching on the craft of the plays, with a side-glance at some of the characters in the novels, and a brief reference to the poems.

A book might be devoted to the artistry which went to the making of Galsworthy's thirty volumes; he worked in so many forms that merely to list them is to excite surprise at his versatility: the very short story, the short story, the long-short story—of which *A Stoic, The Apple Tree,* and *The Indian Summer of a Forsyte* are the high lights; the novel, the trilogy, the trilogy of trilogies (for *The Forsyte Saga, A Modern Comedy,* and the last three novels form a whole); the sketch, the poem, the short play, the long play, the well-made play, the episodic play, the fantasy, the essay, the address. Critical appraisal I leave to others. My purpose has been to reveal the man as shown in his life and work, and only in so far as I have personally contacted them. Naturally, I have not avoided references to his skill when they seemed appropriate to my purpose, nor failed to note such limitations in his art as seemed to me significant; and it is not possible to quote copiously from his books without provoking admiration for the flexibility and limpid clarity of his unaffected prose.

FOREWORD

A word on this matter of quotations is due here. As nothing irritates me more than a page broken by inset quotations and sprinkled with what are inaccurately called inverted commas, I have decided to take the law into my own hands and whenever possible dispense with these conventional acknowledgments of source. When my quotation is taken directly from the mouth of a character, I have in most cases used the accustomed quotation-marks; in other cases I have allowed the context to declare when the words are Galsworthy's and when my own. This has permitted me to change tenses and the like without being compelled to justify myself by pouring out a spate of inverted and elevated commas. One fanciful example will, I hope, secure forgiveness for this breach of the rules. If Galsworthy had written: "She went home, opened the door, took off her hat, and waited for her mother" and I wished, for the sake of fluency in reading, to quote this passage in the present tense, I should have remorselessly written it thus:

She goes home, opens the door, takes off her hat, and waits for her mother,

wantonly avoiding the usual method, which would be:

"She" goes "home," opens "the door," takes "off her hat, and" waits "for her mother."

H. O.

THE TYPICAL ENGLISHMAN

THE TYPICAL ENGLISHMAN

IT has always puzzled me that Galsworthy who, more than any novelist of his generation, attacked the very foundations of English society, should have been alluded to with parrot-like frequency as "the typical Englishman." In his lifetime the label was attached with such conviction that nothing seemed able to dislodge it, and when he died hundreds of journalists, as if in collusion, repeated the pronouncement as though it were axiomatic. That it would be difficult to imagine Galsworthy as anything but English is true, but this for negative rather than positive reasons. If, endowed with the gifts which were peculiar to him, he had been born a Frenchman, an Italian, an American, a German, a Russian, he would have expressed himself differently, exchanging the limitations imposed by English tradition for those of his native land, but the essential Galsworthy would have remained the same, and to describe the sum of his gifts and character as typically English seems to me as inept as it would be to docket Shakespeare in a similarly comprehensive fashion. Galsworthy had certain traits—manners, rather than mental or emotional characteristics—which stamped him English, traits which he shared with English lawyers, parsons, shop-keepers and policemen, but his personality in the wider sense was no more typically English than Goethe's was typically German: it was *sui generis*.

Whatever may be meant by the words "typically English," there is no doubt whatever that Galsworthy, from the moment that he became aware of his social conscience—the tenderest ever given to man—used his pen as a flail to attack everything in English society which conflicted with his sense of justice. Side by side with his appreciation of everything that is admirable in English institutions and in the English attitude, we find an unceasing criticism of England's more flagrant failings.

Mr. Desmond MacCarthy, in an article not otherwise remarkable for clarity, very cogently pigeonholed the characteristic faults of the French and the Irish, and then proceeded to diagnose the English. "English faults have no such precise abusive names," he wrote; "nevertheless they are disgusting. They can be indicated: an incurable determination in the face of truth, honour, art, to have things both ways (the nearest curse-word for this is hypocrisy, though that is far too crude), and an impenetrable self-complacency—smugness for short, smugness moral and intellectual." Nobody could have been more painfully aware of these failings than Galsworthy, and nobody has more subtly exposed them than he. As his aim was to depict life with some verisimilitude, he did not, like the creators of Tartuffe and Pecksniff, identify his characters with particular blemishes. He wanted to show men and women in the round, with their failings and their qualities, some of which are the obverse of the others, leaving the virtues to make their own claims on the reader's approval and the failings to inspire the deserved repugnance. His practice was to attempt to understand, and even when describing the fault, not to condemn the sinner. There is a handful of characters in his plays and novels who seem to lack any redeeming qualities, but they are so few that in a world as thickly populated as Galsworthy's they may be safely left out of the count. The rest of his offenders have mitigating characteristics: their offences are often unintentional, due to stupidity or to a lack of imagination, or, being inherent in their mental make-up, are no more to be condemned than a hare-lip; or perhaps they are the unwilling instruments of institutions. One who to-day behaves with blind callousness may to-morrow show an unexpected tenderness; the Soames who aches to the soles of his shoes because Irene repulses him, snaps at any criticism of her from others; the Reverend Hussell Barter, possessive, narrow and self-centred, releases a thirsty tethered horse and leads it to the water . . . and faintly resents the absence of gratitude in the poor beast. Galsworthy, in fact, had little use for the black and white psychology of conventional fiction, was profoundly convinced of the fundamental good intentions of most men and women, and while criticising actions, conventions, and institutions, left life itself to deal with the evil-doers, who by their own deeds set in motion the machinery which "punished" them, if one must use such a word to describe the automatic process of sowing and reaping.

From the moment when Shelton, after a long absence in the East, revisits his native England and beholds the Island Pharisees who inhabit it—the curious smugness of the passers-by, the utterly unending bustle, the fearful medley of miserable, over-driven women, and full-fed men with leering, bull-beef eyes—Galsworthy enters the lists not only against those sins of smugness and hypocrisy which Mr. MacCarthy considers are our most typical faults, but against every flaw in the English character and in the English social system, whether typical or sporadic. English institutions and habits of mind, the English country and the English capital, English weaknesses and English strength—these were the foreground, the background and the middle-distance of the Galsworthy world, the atmosphere in which his English men and women lived and moved and had their being, and if, on balance, England seems a fair and pleasant land, and English people, on balance, fair and pleasant people, it is not because Galsworthy attempted to paint a prettier picture than his eyes beheld, but because, perhaps, to the impersonal eye, these things are so. In matters small and large Galsworthy saw us clearly and honestly and spoke us fair.

Let us examine the evidence and confound those who, seeking for an explanation of Galsworthy's popularity in his own country, declare that he drew a picture which revealed only such faults as the Englishman is willing cheerfully to admit, so long as his more serious failings are not uncovered. (By the way, could the popularity of Mr. Sinclair Lewis, Dickens, Thackeray, Tolstoy, Anatole France and Dostoievsky be similarly explained?)

In *The Island Pharisees* Galsworthy was more prone to pronounce judgments *ex cathedra* than in more mature work; in later novels he allowed his mind to be transmuted in the alembic of his characters' personality. His rather shadowy heroine, Antonia, he tells us, belonged to the most civilised division of the race most civilised in all the world, whose creed is: "Let us love and hate, let us work and marry, but let us never give ourselves away; to give ourselves away is to leave a mark, and that is past forgiveness. Let

our lives be like our faces, free from every kind of
wrinkle, even those of laughter; in this way alone
can we be really civilized." And later, Shelton con-
tends that in England we've mislaid the recipe of
life. . . . Pleasure's a lost art. We don't get drunk,
we're ashamed of love, and as to beauty, we've lost
the eye for it. . . . As to thought, we think so much
of what our neighbours think that we never think at
all.

This fear of emotion, or at least of the expression of
it, which marks off the English from the rest of the
world, was again and again held up to mild ridicule
by Galsworthy. George Pendyce's creed (*The
Country House*) permitted the show of no emotion.
Excellent sportsman that he was, even when beaten
there was enjoyment to be had out of the imper-
turbability with which he could take that beating,
out of a sense of superiority to men not quite so
sportsmanlike as himself. Poor George! An emotional creature, stifling everything for good form's
sake! The gall and bitterness which surged into his
brain when he was defeated on the racecourse could
find no outlet. There is no place, no corner, on a
racecourse where a man may show his heart. George
did but lay his forehead against the velvet of his
horse's muzzle, and for one short second hold it
there—rejoicing, no doubt, in the thought that a
horse was a dumb animal and could not give him
away! Even Margery Pendyce, who had been known
to give way to emotion, more habitually suppressed
it. No reader of *The Country House*, having succumbed
to the charms of that gracious lady, is likely to forget
that night when she lay awake by her sleeping husband's side in the darkness which covered the
emotions that overwhelmed her and sanctioned the

temporary suspension of the instinct of a lady which commonly governed her behaviour. This instinct, so elastic and so subtle, so interwoven of consideration for others and consideration for herself, so old, so very old, wrapped her from all eyes, like a suit of armour of the finest chain. The night must have been black indeed when she took that off and lay without it in the darkness.

Stephen, in *Fraternity*, is perhaps the extreme type of emotion-hating Englishman. In him there was a horror of emotion amounting almost to disease and when Thyme, his grown-up daughter, moved beyond the power of restraint, shows her feelings, he receives a shock. It would have been difficult to say when he had last shown emotion; perhaps not since Thyme was born, and even then not to anyone except himself, having first locked the door, and then walked up and down with his teeth almost meeting in the mouthpiece of his favourite pipe. Educated at a public school and Cambridge, Stephen was very civilised, with that bone-deep decency, that dislike of violence, nowhere so prevalent as in the upper classes of a country whose settled institutions are as old as its roads, or the walls which insulate its parks. Stephen was even unmoved by the call of a Spring wind which wanted to tell him of the million flowers it had fertilised, the million leaves uncurled . . . and how into men's hearts its scent had driven a million longings and sweet pains . . . for Stephen, like all men of culture and neat habits, took Nature only at those moments when he had gone out to take her, and of her wild heart he had a secret fear.

The English disinclination to give any sign of deep feeling is nowhere more evident than between members of the same family—an idiosyncrasy, this, which

JOHN GALSWORTHY—probably 1915.

To face p. 22.

foreigners find unintelligible. Between Soames and his father there existed a fairly deep affection, but the outward relationship was marked by a lack of sentiment peculiarly Forsytean. Perhaps they regarded one another as an investment; certainly they were solicitous of each other's welfare, glad of each other's company. They never exchanged two words upon the more intimate problems of life, or revealed in each other's presence the existence of any deep feeling. Something beyond the power of word-analysis bound them together, something hidden deep in the fibre of nations and families—for blood, they say, is thicker than water—and neither of them was a cold-blooded man. One generation of Forsytes succeeds another in Galsworthy's chronicles, and though young Forsytes may powder their noses and salve their lips in public, nevertheless their emotions are held in leash. "It's airing them that kills feelings," says Holly.

There is an exquisitely humorous passage in *Fraternity* which, with the necessary exaggeration, sums up the English reserve. Hilary is taking a walk with the dog Miranda. He sits down; and underneath his seat, Miranda found what she had been looking for all her life. It had no smell, made no movement, was pale-grey in colour, like herself. It had no hair that she could find; its tail was like her own; it took no liberties, was silent, had no passions, committed her to nothing. Standing a few inches from its head, closer than she had ever been of her free will to any dog, she smelt its smell-lessness with a long, delicious snuffling, wrinkling up the skin of her forehead, and through her upturned eyes her little moonlight soul looked forth. "How unlike you are," she seemed to say, "to all the other dogs I know. I would love to live with you. Shall I ever find a dog like you again? 'The latest—sterilised cloth—see white label underneath: 4s. 3d.'" Suddenly she slithered out her slender grey-pink tongue and licked its nose. The creature moved a little way and stopped. Miranda saw that it had wheels. She lay down close to it, for she knew it was the perfect dog.

That there is something admirable as well as something absurd in this distrust of emotion nobody would deny; if it makes for repressions and unresolved complexes, it also makes for self-control and a concern for other people's sensibilities, and in poking fun at it, Galsworthy does not omit to allow it whatever credit may be due to it. To dub it hypocrisy would be too severe and also inexact: rather is it the fear of ridicule and an aspect of pride.

It is more worth while to tilt at self-righteousness, hypocrisy and smugness, especially, perhaps, when the wounds we inflict on others bleed from our own veins. Galsworthy's mature method was not to pillory these failings by naming them, but by showing them in being. From time to time (but rarely) he threw out in passing a phrase like "all men save hypocrites and Englishmen" (*The Dark Flower*); from time to time a character like Felix in *The Free-lands* would exclaim at a moment of exasperation: "Our smug attitude is odious" and even discourse didactically to his brother Stephen in this wise: "The Mallorings, I've not the slightest doubt, believe it their duty to look after the morals of those who live on their property. There are three things to be said about that: You can't make people moral by adopting the attitude of the schoolmaster. It implies that they consider themselves more moral than their neighbours. It's a theory so convenient to their security that they would be exceptionally good people if they did not adopt it; but from your account, they are not so much exceptionally as just typically good people. What you call their sense of duty, Stanley, is really their sense of self-preservation coupled with their sense of superiority."

But more often Galsworthy's method is elliptical: self-righteousness and its offspring are allowed to speak for themselves. General Pendyce prays every night to God that the Liberals won't get in. Behind his personal interest his ancestors had drilled into him the impossibility of imagining that he did not stand for the welfare of his country. His brother Horace, reading the lesson in church, hypnotised by the sound of his own voice, has a little running accompaniment of thought: "This lesson is well read by me Horace Pendyce. I am Horace Pendyce— Horace Pendyce. Amen. Horace Pendyce!" And, fully convinced that he is serving his country and his God, he lives according to the unexpounded creed: "I believe in my father, and his father, and his father's father, the makers and keepers of my estate and I believe in myself and my son and my son's son. And I believe that we have made the country, and shall keep the country what it is. And I believe in the Public Schools, and especially in the Public School that I was at. And I believe in my social equals and the country house, and in things as they are, for ever and ever. Amen."

Smugness of a concentrated order is to be found in the Mallorings (*The Freelands*); in their attitude to their social inferiors and to those who profess views other than their own. Mildred Malloring believed implicitly in her own righteousness, and however much she might be shaken by circumstances and antagonism, equilibrium would eventually be restored because that belief was fundamental. From very childhood she had felt that the essence of her own goodness, the essence of her duty in life, was the doing of "good" to others; from very childhood she had never doubted that she was in a position to do this, and that those to whom she did good, although they might kick against it as inconvenient, must admit that it *was* their "good." The thought: "They don't admit that I am superior" had never even occurred to her, so completely was she unself-conscious, in her convinced superiority.

The smugness of Stephen Dallison has been alluded to; his wife Cecilia ran him pretty close. Contact with the "lower classes," except from a plane of patronage, was, to her, contamination. When her brother-in-law Hilary appeared to be entangled with the little model, the affair was to her "sordid." She used this word instinctively. It had come into her mind at once. The whole affair disturbed her ideals of virtue and good taste—that particular mental atmosphere mysteriously, inevitably woven round the soul by the conditions of special breeding and special life. If, then, this affair were real it was sordid, and if it were sordid it was repellent to suppose that her family could be mixed up in it; but her people *were* mixed up in it; therefore it must be—nonsense!

There is also, it may be confessed, something smug in the sense of superiority which colours Miltoun's make-up (*The Patrician*). On the whole he is a sympathetic character; his deep sincerity, his profound sense of duty, his imagination and idealism, not to mention his capacity to suffer for love's sake, all speak in his favour. Wealth in its more vulgar manifestations he despised, but although the author of his being declares that there was nothing of the common Pharisee about Miltoun, he does not absolve him from an intense and growing conviction of his capacity for leadership, of a spiritual superiority to those whom he desired to benefit, and in this he revealed something which, if not smug, came perilously near to priggishness.

Smugness and hypocrisy are often less the effect of a conscious desire to have it both ways than of a crass inability to see that there is more than one way. An unconscious failing is no less irritating than one which is conscious, but it is, alas, less easily to be condemned. Even Viscount Harbinger, in the same book, narrow almost to vanishing point, acts according to his lights and claims a certain sympathetic appreciation in the reader. As Galsworthy says, it would have been unfair to call his enthusiasm for social reform spurious. It was real enough in its way, and did certainly testify that he was not altogether lacking either in imagination or good-heartedness. But it was over and overlaid with the public-school habit—that peculiar, extraordinary English habit, so powerful and beguiling that it becomes a second nature stronger than the first—of relating everything in the Universe to the standards and prejudices of a single class. Since practically all his intimate associates were immersed in it, he was naturally not in the least conscious of this habit. It is a tribute to Galsworthy's genius that he is able to see a man and his prejudices clearly and make him likeable without concealing or sentimentalising any of his shortcomings. His works are rich in such miracles, the greatest of which is, of course, Soames Forsyte, who becomes more and more likeable as he grows older and we get to know more about him, in spite of characteristics which must have been as repugnant to Galsworthy as they are to us. The fact is that Soames is so vividly realised from within and from without that we are raised to the position of a creator who, knowing everything, forgives everything.

But it is unnecessary to multiply instances: the plays and the novels teem with them.

More irritating to our foreign neighbours than even our hypocrisy (and allied to it) is the closeness which leaves them guessing at our intentions. They credit us with a Machiavellian cleverness which has little relation to a *modus operandi* more aptly described as muddling-through, and, like Soames' French wife Annette, accuse us of always waiting to see which way the cat will jump. "And why shouldn't we?" retorts Soames. "Rushing into things that you'll have to rush out of!" Sir James Faggart (*The Silver Spoon*) rubs in the same charge. "Knowledge in Europe . . . of what England will or will not do in given cases is most important. And they've never had it. *Perfide Albion!* Heh! We always wait till the last moment to declare our policy. Great mistake. Gives the impression that we serve Time—which, with our democratic system, by the way, we generally do."

This, of course, is a desire to have things both ways, an over-cautiousness which clings to dogmas that have ceased to have any meaning for us, lest there should, after all, be something in them, and linked up to those prayers which come so glibly from unbelievers when they want anything. Most of all does this national characteristic show itself in sexual matters. It might almost be said that in this Soames is the average Englishman, who has his full share of the faun but is careful to keep the fact hidden. Like most of his family, Soames was secretive in matters of sex; no Forsyte talked sex, or liked to hear others talk it; and when they felt its call, they gave no outward sign. It is significant, and shows Galsworthy's sureness in characterisation, that Fleur, half-French as she is, has none of this self-deluding attitude to sex. She desires Jon physically, and makes a dead set at him until she gets him, notwithstanding her own husband and Jon's wife; nothing, certainly not Jon, could resist this primitive demand of hers. Meantime, and later, she has no false delicacy about living with her husband. Fastidious recoilings from unloved husbands of which she read in old-fashioned novels, and of which she knew her father's first wife, Irene, had been guilty, seemed to her rather ludicrous.

Self-righteousness in war-time is not a prerogative of the English. In another chapter I shall endeavour to give some account of Galsworthy's feelings about war and that aspect of the subject will be touched on there. But although imperialism is not a monopoly of the British, nor Chauvinism our invention, both are sufficiently closely identified with us to warrant a critic of England in attacking them in us. Galsworthy's opinion in such matters was conditioned, as usual, by his keen sense of justice, and he was always particularly insensed by the hypocrisy which permitted us to claim as idealistic, a policy which was primarily prompted by self-interest. *The Forest* is the only one of his works which is exclusively devoted to this subject, but is by no means the only one in which his attitude is made clear. The forest itself symbolises the great imperialist jungle which takes its toll of men—the jungle law which prevails in the politico-commercial world. The individuals concerned in the marauding and plunder which play such an important part in empire-building are not all self-interested: often they are unimaginative tools in the hands of the unscrupulous, sometimes men whose instinct for adventure outvies any other consideration, and often, needless to say, they are convinced believers that it is beneficial to the human race as a whole that the British flag should be planted in as many profitable places as possible. Bravery, enterprise, enthusiasm and energy, and other admirable qualities, are frequently characteristic of those who engage in these adventures: it is a pity that hypocrisy so often joins company with them, and that the ironical reply of the Arab Samehda to the high idealistic claims of the British should have any justification:

SAMEHDA. I born Zanzibar—I know white men —come from across sea—take country—ivory— slave—all that belong Arab. Belgian—English —German. And all say: "Serve Allah! Free slave." All steal from Arab.

STROOD. Arab stole first from black men, Samehda.

SAMEHDA. Then Arab keep if can; white men take if can. Arab serve Allah too.

More explicitly, Galsworthy's scepticism finds expression in *The Island Pharisees*. "How can progress be imposed on nations from without?" asks Shelton of a returned Indian civil servant. "Give me a single example of a nation, or an individual, for that matter, who's ever done any good without having worked up to it from within. . . . We take peoples entirely different from our own, and stop their natural development by substituting a civilisation grown for our own use. . . . Should we go on administering India if it were a dead loss? No. Well, to talk about administering the country for the purpose of pocketing money is cynical, and there's generally some truth in cynicism; but to talk about the administration of a country by which we profit, as if it were a great and good thing, is cant. I hit you in the wind for the benefit of myself—all right: law of Nature; but to say it does you good at the same time is beyond me. . . . We always think our standards best for the whole world. It's a capital belief for us."

From this point of view I do not think that Galsworthy ever travelled very far.

MAN *VERSUS* SOCIETY

MAN *VERSUS* SOCIETY

MAN *versus* Society, the free mind *versus* the conventional; in a word, the individual *versus* the mass: this theme was very persistently in Galsworthy's mind. By no means denying that conventions were an inevitable corollary of human society, having a certain affection for traditional institutions, and a temperamental leaning towards orderliness, he had, like Shelton in *The Island Pharisees*, an ingrained overtenderness of soul which made him painfully aware of the sufferings wrought upon the individual who by nature or by daring comes in conflict with Society. He believed utterly in the right of the individual to free expression, but that side of him which had been developed by legal training knew that the State, to maintain its prestige, must prevent the individual from acting in any way which it deems subversive. This dilemma will exist as long as government of any kind exists, whether parliamentary, dictatorship, socialist or bolshevist; and even if, in some remote future, human beings were to find that they could survive without government, the problem of the individual *versus* the mass would still persist, however greatly it were mitigated by enhanced tolerance. Tolerance is, indeed, the saving grace which Galsworthy was always applauding—that policy of Live-and-let-live invented by man, which has no place, apparently, in Nature's own scheme. Mirror to the

35

JOHN GALSWORTHY

world its stupidities and cruelties, and the world, ashamed, may heed and mend: that was one of Galsworthy's aims, and the one which most determined his method. Nobody was more clearly aware than he of Society's decree "Conform or perish," but the weight of his sympathy was always with the victim of the decree and not with the Society which imposed it.

"INEXORABLE INCOMPATIBILITY . . ."

In another chapter I have shown how deeply Galsworthy was moved by the misery of ill-matched sexual alliances. Such misery might be prevented from becoming tragic if the law of divorce were other than it is. Soames, who had been living apart from Irene for years, could not be divorced unless *fresh* misconduct were proved, the Law demanding further "immorality" before allowing two incompatible persons voluntarily to go their separate ways. "Two unhappy persons must not seem to agree to be parted," said the lawyer in *The Country House*. "One must be believed to desire to keep hold of the other, and must pose as an injured person." The Law does not claim the unfailing allegiance even of lawyers. Listen to Paramor: "Don't let these matters come into court. If there is anything you can do to prevent it, do it. If your pride stands in the way, put it in your pocket. If your sense of truth stands in the way, forget it. Between personal delicacy and our law of divorce there is no relation; between absolute truth and our law of divorce there is no relation. I repeat, don't let these matters come into court. Innocent and guilty, you will all suffer; the innocent will suffer more than the guilty, and nobody will benefit." The bitterness expressed here, in one of his

36

earliest books, is echoed with if anything greater vehemence in his last, *Over the River*.

The poor caught up in the machinery of the law are particularly pathetic. Man and wife, mutually at loggerheads, form a pact when faced with the blind enmity of the Law. So it was with the Hughs (*Fraternity*) when the man was on trial for assaulting his wife. Whatever their grievances against one another, against this impersonal judge they seemed to enter into a sudden league. A look passed between them. It was not friendly, it had no appeal; but it sufficed. There seemed to be expressed in it the knowledge bred of immemorial experience and immemorial time: This Law before which we stand was not made by us! As dogs, when they hear the crack of a far whip, will shrink, and in their whole bearing show wary quietude, so Hughs and Mrs. Hughs, confronted by the questionings of Law, made only such answers as could be dragged from them.

In *The Silver Box* a similar situation shows the Law in an even more unfavourable light. Incidentally this play—one of the author's best—is sufficient answer to the charge frequently directed against Galsworthy, that he carries impartiality so far that his situations end in stalemate. Here, as in numerous other cases where judgment is truthfully possible, the author shows clearly enough where his sympathies lie. He puts before us a rich man and a poor man charged with theft, both of them tipsy at the time, both of them thieves by accident and not by design: the rich man is wangled free of the consequences of his peccadillo; the poor man goes to prison. The chief sufferer, the poor man's wife, is completely innocent of any misdemeanour. Galsworthy's impartiality is shown not by putting everybody in the right, but by making the instruments of the law behave like human beings, without vindictiveness. It is the machine, Law, which is at fault, and it is futile to argue with a machine. Change it, or scrap it.

Galsworthy's reputed impartiality is also shown, or should we say exploded, in *Justice*, when the weak but chivalrous Falder is sentenced to three years' hard labour for altering the amount of a cheque from £9 to £90 in order to provide money for taking an unhappily married woman to South America. Whether the sentence is excessive or not is neither here nor there: it was passed in accordance with the Law, which, the Judge informs us, is a majestic edifice, sheltering all of us, each stone of which rests on another. But the crime committed by Falder against Society is venial in comparison with the crime committed by Society against humanity. To handle a weakling, driven in a moment of stress to offend against the laws of Property, as if he were a tough criminal, hardened in sinning, is as unjust as it is stupid. And this Galsworthy reveals, with so much aptness and truth that the effect of the play on an audience is overwhelming.

Incidentally the play, by staging a scene in a prison cell, where Falder is shown serving part of his sentence in solitary confinement, is said to have led to certain reforms in prison regulations. But those who take comfort from this thought must not imagine that solitary confinement has been abolished from English prisons: it is still one of the normal features of our prison régime.

The machinery of Law fascinated Galsworthy and his work contains far more significant allusions to it

Photo: Stage Photo Co.

A SCENE FROM " JUSTICE."

COLIN CLIVE as " Falder "; LAWRENCE HANRAY as " Cokeson ";
MARGARETTA SCOTT as " Ruth."

To face p. 38.

than can be mentioned here. He turned the knowledge gained through his legal training to excellent
uses; it served equally well his artistic powers and his
social conscience; and it provided him with many of
his most dramatic situations and effective scenes.
If he could have brought himself to be the servant of
an institution of which, in many of its manifestations,
he thoroughly disapproved, he would have made a
perfect judge. I was always impressed, at the many
committee meetings over which I have seen him
preside, by his capacity for grasping the pros and
cons of a proposition, weighing them dispassionately
and pronouncing a judgment so astute that it nearly
always went without criticism. But at these meetings
he had to decide, not what was legal according to
the Laws of the land, but what was just, expedient,
and wise in the given circumstances. "Between
justice and what was just," as Dinny Charwell
found, "what inexorable incompatibility!"

"*THE PACK SPIRIT*" . . .

Galsworthy was not a politically minded man in
spite of his keen interest in political measures and his
astuteness in his judgment of them. No party
claimed his definite allegiance and he rarely exercised
his right to vote. An exception was when he came
up from the country especially to vote for the
National Government in 1931. I remember his
surprise at my astonishment that he should have
succumbed to this particular temptation. He felt
that the situation was desperate, he told me, and
believed that a sincere attempt was about to be
made to cope with it; but I am afraid I was not convinced. Having no political *nous*, however, but only
a handful of political principles that serve as a

touchstone by which to judge all political problems, I did not pursue the subject. Instead, I listened to the details of an emigration scheme for dealing with the problem of the Unemployed, which he propounded in detail.

Broadly, he believed in democracy, but the term bore for him no mystical significance and carried with it no patent of infallibility. Democracy was at its best a cumbersome method for the attainment of approximate equity, and although he believed that public sentiment was generally ahead of the Law, *Vox populi vox Dei* is not a dictum to which he would have readily subscribed: he was too keenly conscious of the hardships which individuals are apt to suffer under a majority dictatorship. It is in the nature of men and angels to pursue with death such birds as are uncommon, such animals as are rare, he said; and Society has no use for those so uncut to its pattern as to be practically unconscious of its existence. Democracy, functioning through the ballot-box, its zeal funnelled into a small stream of much diluted reforms, is not a very formidable force, but the People, unrestrained and expressing itself corporately, is capable of sinking far beneath the level of its lowest unit and becoming a terrifying, blind power.

Before this monster Galsworthy recoiled, knowing it to be of all the enemies of progress the most pernicious and least easy to overcome. His novels, and particularly his plays, offer much evidence of this conviction. The individual may be reached through reasoning—the mob, never. Mob sentiment is so frequently sentimentality; mob indignation, the ferocity of an animal bilked of its prey. "The mob!" exclaims Miltoun (*The Patrician*) when he discovered that he had secured some party advantage by the characteristically shady tactics of his election agent —"How I loathe it! I hate its mean stupidities, I hate the sound of its voice, and the look on its face— it's so ugly, it's so little." With the spiritual pride and the conviction of superiority which dominated the life of Miltoun and contributed so bitterly to its tragedy, Galsworthy had little in common; his sense of humour and the breadth of his vision saved him from condemning men while disapproving and hating the things they did. But he would have shrunk, no less than Miltoun did, from being judged by mob law. Miltoun in a crowd, watching the drifters pass by, was filled with contempt for the average or common when Galsworthy would have been moved to pity or sympathy, but he would not have failed to observe that they looked soft, soggy, without pride or will, as though they knew life was too much for them, and had shamefully accepted the fact, and he would probably have felt, as Miltoun did, that they obviously needed to be told what they might do, and which way they should go; they would accept orders as they accepted their work, or pleasures. For over and over again Galsworthy emphasised his conviction that in the progress of civilisation the individual far outvalued the mass. The policeman in *Saint's Progress* attributes the ill-deeds of the Germans in the war to "the vicious way they're brought up, of actin' in the mass; that's made 'em such a crool lot," he says. "I see a good bit of crowds in my profession, and I've a very low opinion of them. Crowds are the most blunderin' blighted things that ever was. They're like an angry woman with a bandage over her eyes, an' you can't have anything more dangerous than that."

The Mob, which it is interesting to recall was written in 1913 and produced before the Great War, gives in concentrated dramatic form some of Galsworthy's profoundest convictions: the importance of the individual and his inalienable right to act in obedience to his conscience; the blind tyranny of the mob stimulated not by principles but by fear and the cruder forms of patriotism and by hatred of anything which refuses to conform to its standards; the instinct to hound, isolate, and if possible destroy the uncommon and strange. The country is at war; Stephen More believes that his country is in the wrong. He is a member of Parliament and publicly expresses and continues to express his views. It is the unforgivable sin. A country at war will countenance no dissentients. The will of the country must be one will. Everybody turns against him, even his wife, who cannot digest the notion that a man should follow his deepest convictions even though they conflicted with what she regarded as his duty to her. The mob, ever eager for a victim, hounds down Stephen More with accumulating venom, and he is killed in a brawl. Before he dies, however, he ex-expresses his opinion of the mob in one of the bitterest passages in all Galsworthy:

"You are here by the law that governs the action of all mobs—the law of Force," he says in a quiet voice. "By that law, you can do what you like to this body of mine. . . . You—Mob—are the most contemptible thing under the sun. When you walk the street, God goes in. . . . My fine friends, I'm not afraid of you. You've forced your way into my house, and you've asked me to speak. Put up with the truth for once! You are the thing that pelts the weak; kicks women; howls down free speech. This to-day, that to-morrow. Brain—you have none.

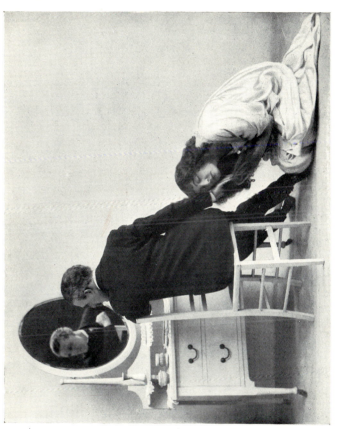

"THE MOB." MILTON ROSMER AND IRENE ROOKE.
Gaiety Theatre, Manchester, March 30, 1914.

To face p. 42.

Spirit—not the ghost of it! If you're not meanness, there's no such thing. If you're not cowardice, there is no cowardice. Patriotism—there are two kinds—that of our soldiers, and this of mine. You have neither. . . My country is not yours. Mine is that great country which shall never take toll from the weakness of others."

On all fours with *The Mob* is *A Bit o' Love*. Once again the hero—Michael Strangway, a country curate—is at odds with Society. His wife is in love with another man and he allows her to go to her lover, because, although the loss of her breaks his heart, believing in the teachings of Christ, he will not cast a stone. Such conduct is interpreted by all who hear of it as cowardice, weak-kneed complacence, and unmanliness; in every sphere of society he is reviled and the mob would have its way with him. Like Stephen More, Strangway keeps his soul alive by standing firm to his faith; unlike More, he does not meet with death, but, through suffering, reaches the conviction that he must learn to love all living things—even his enemies, even those who revile him.

If the mob in its rancour, fear and scorn is petty and contemptible, it is scarcely more admirable in its jubilation. From the joy which broke from the populace when Mafeking was relieved one of the most scathing English verbs—to maffick—came into existence. Soames (*In Chancery*) wandering into Regent Street one night in May found himself in the midst of the most amazing crowd he had ever seen; a shrieking, whistling, dancing, jostling, grotesque and formidably jovial crowd, with false noses, and mouth organs, penny whistles and long feathers, every appanage of idiocy, as it seemed to him.

Mafeking! Of course, it had been relieved! Good! But was that an excuse? Who were these people, what were they, where had they come from into the West End? His face was tickled, his ears whistled into. Girls cried: "Keep your hair on, stucco!" A youth so knocked off his top-hat that he recovered it with difficulty. Crackers were exploding beneath his nose, between his feet. He was bewildered, exasperated, offended. This stream of people came from every quarter, as if impulse had unlocked flood-gates, let flow waters of whose existence he had heard, perhaps, but believed in never. This, then, was the populace, the innumerable living negation of gentility and Forsyteism; this was—egad!—Democracy! It stank, yelled, was hideous!

Seen thus with the eyes of Soames, smelled, as it were, with his over-fastidious nose, the mob puts on certain virtues; but Soames did not at this time stand exclusively for the less admirable characteristics of his class: he also stood for a certain decency in behaviour, a certain desirable restraint and reticence, and it is not unprofitable to share his sensations as he looked at the cauldron with the lid off, hardly able to believe his scorching eyes. He found the whole thing unspeakable. These people had no restraint. And not unnaturally, perhaps, they seemed to think him funny. There were such swarms of them, rude, coarse, laughing—and what laughter! Nothing sacred to them! He shouldn't be surprised if they began to break windows. This was serious, he reflected—might come to anything. To-day the crowd was cheerful, but some day they would come in different mood. . . . But more than dread, he felt a deep surprise. They were hysterical—it wasn't English.

"When all the packs of all the world are out for blood," philosophy must retire and bide the time when sanity shall have been restored; for if there is one thing more certain than that the mob can be aroused to insensate activity, it is that, its energy spent, it will sink into apathy.

"CURRENTS OF INK . . ."

As the medium through which the less admirable qualities of the people were expressed and their meaner appetites catered for, Galsworthy had no love for the Press. Its habit of stressing the unimportant at the expense of the essential infuriated him; its inaccuracy irritated him, and he was contemptuous of the callousness which permitted it to pierce the privacy of people's lives. He himself carried the avoidance of publicity to an almost unreasonable point. This sprang from that genuine modesty which found it hard to accept the fact that a man who had attained his celebrity was a legitimate object of curiosity to his readers. Mr. Henry W. Nevinson—if I may digress for a moment—was once driving with him from The Hague to Rotterdam. It was at one of the international congresses of the P.E.N. "Our car arrived half an hour before the rest of the party," said Mr. Nevinson. "A lot of photographers were waiting on the steps of the Town Hall, obviously waiting for him alone. As a fellow-journalist, I pitied them, and urged him to leave the car and announce himself so as to save their time. But no persuasion touched him. He leant back in the car and refused to move until the common crowd came up, and he could be lost in it." Diffidence rather than modesty is perhaps the word to express this very typical behaviour of Galsworthy, of which I could give many similar examples. No doubt it explained in part his peculiarly profound understanding of the pain inflicted upon sensitive people when their intimate affairs are paraded in the Press and courts.

The bitterest embodiment of his feelings on this subject are to be found in *The Show*, in which the Press is pilloried unmercifully for the part it played in digging up irrelevant facts that caused intense suffering to half a dozen entirely innocent people. Journalists—for whom no one ever has a good word—are trounced unmercifully; they are referred to as ghoulish harpies and cats who feed a gaping public on any garbage of devil's gossip that will sell their paper—thus Colonel Roland; and it would be hard to find an extenuating circumstance in their favour. To them the whole thing is "news", and the more unsavoury it can be made to appear, the more acceptable will their "copy" be. Having attained that divine detachment known only to journalists and judges, the human beings sacrificed to their activities are no more to them than sheep grazing on a Wiltshire plain are to a seller of mutton in Clapham. None of the facts so skilfully unearthed were needed for "justice." The young airman who had committed suicide was irrevocably dead; to sully his reputation, to delve into the private lives of those dear to him and inflict shame and dismay upon them, was surely to hold an unduly exalted view of the duty of the Press to the public. "The Press gets all the blame for the natural instincts of mankind," protests the Editor. "I don't care what they say, curiosity is the greatest thing in the world. Somebody's got to stand up for the man in the street. Why *shouldn't* he know?"

A passage in one of his later works—*Maid in*

46

JOHN GALSWORTHY, JO VAN AMMERS-KÜLLER AND MRS. GALSWORTHY, OUTSIDE THE TOWN HALL, ROTTERDAM, JUNE 22, 1931. MR. H. W. NEVINSON BRINGS UP THE REAR.

To face p. 46.

Waiting—displays an acidity which is rare in his writings and shows how deeply ingrained into his system was Galsworthy's resentment of this side of the Press. I quote verbatim: "Every reader of a newspaper felt that the more he or she heard about what was doubtful, sensational, and unsavoury, the better for his or her soul. One knew that, without coroner's inquests, there would often be no published inquiry at all into sensational death; and never two inquiries. If, then, in place of no inquiry one could always have one inquiry, and in place of one inquiry sometimes have two inquiries, how much pleasanter! The dislike which one had for being nosey disappeared the moment one got into a crowd. The nosier one could be in a crowd, the happier one felt. And the oftener one could find room in a Coroners' Court, the greater the thankfulness to Heaven. 'Praise God from whom all blessings flow' could never go up more fervently than from the hearts of such as had been privileged to find seats at an inquiry about death. For an inquiry about death nearly always meant the torture of the living, and than that was anything more calculated to give pleasure?"

As far back as *In Chancery*, some fourteen years earlier, Soames dismissed the newspapers as a pushing lot, pretending to guard the public's morals while corrupting them with their beastly reports.

But if Galsworthy was appalled by the voracity of the Press in the matter of salacious news-items, he was no less appalled by its neglect of matters of serious national or international concern. In a letter to me in December 1931 he expressed his disgust at the indifference shown to an appeal on behalf of political prisoners which, bearing the signatures of most of the greatest names in modern literature, had been circulated to the Press. It is worth while recording the text of the appeal here, for although it was sponsored by the International P.E.N., it was, in fact, drafted by him:

APPEAL TO ALL GOVERNMENTS.

"We, undersigned members or honorary members of the non-political World Association of Writers, called the P.E.N., representing some 4,000 writers in thirty-five countries, respectfully draw the attention of all Governments to the following considerations:

"From time to time the conscience of the World is stirred and shocked by revelations of the ill-treatment in this, that or the other country, of people imprisoned on political or religious grounds. We submit that, in such cases, Governments are specially bound to see that humanity is not violated in the treatment of such prisoners.

"We, further, urge Governments to remember that nothing so provokes the ill-will of the world at large against a given country, as knowledge that political or religious prisoners are ill treated; and that such ill treatment is in these days bound, soon or late, to become matter of common knowledge."

This appeal was signed by Mr. G. K. Chesterton, Mr. John Masefield, Professor Gilbert Murray, Mr. G. Bernard Shaw and Mr. H. G. Wells among other English writers, and by authors of similar eminence in twenty-two countries. It appeared widely in the world's Press, notably in those countries which, though unnamed, were tacitly pilloried. The appearance of such an appeal in all the leading English newspapers would have had a far greater effect upon governments responsible for the ill-treatment of prisoners than the Press, in its modesty, might imagine. It is a regrettable fact—and one of many which may have helped to build up Galsworthy's dislike of the Press—that scarcely half a dozen newspapers in this country were willing to give the few inches of space necessary for printing the appeal.

*   *   *   *   *

At no time is the influence of the Press more potent than in war-time: for good or ill it can sway millions who would ordinarily sift it through their own reasoning. War being in progress, the public is apt to surrender its power of reasoning to whatever force is sufficiently masterful to impose its dictatorship; and of the several dictatorships which came into being soon after the outbreak of the Great War, the Press was probably the most powerful. It was virtually the willing mouthpiece of the Government, and among its functions was that of keeping up what was quaintly called the "morale" of the country. The country had to be assured of several things—(a) the righteousness of the Allied cause, (b) the inevitableness of ultimate victory because Right must triumph in the end through whatever reverses it might pass, and (c) the turpitude of the enemy. The first of these was not difficult; the second needed some skill, and the third considerable inventiveness. But inventiveness is not one of the least attributes of journalists, and with a boundless and unresisting field for exploitation, it had unprecedented scope. The hate campaign, as vigorous in other countries as in this, was perhaps the most discreditable of all the unpleasant phenomena in a world of men whose finer feelings had been paralysed by fear, and the Press played a major role in it. This Galsworthy would find it hard to forgive.

It has already been shown how loath he was to draw a journalist possessed of humanity and intelligence. I cannot recall a newspaper man in the Galsworthy world who could be cited as an admirable specimen of modern citizenship, and there are many specimens of journalists who are distinctly below the average standard of human being. The "Press", in *The Foundations*, is a poor creature and expressed only the mildest annoyance when James the Footman says to him: "I've had a grudge against you yellow newspaper boys ever since the war—frothin' up your daily hate, an' makin' the Huns desperate. You nearly took my life five hundred times out there. If you squeal I'm goin' to take yours once—and that'll be enough." And when, later, he is treated with indignity and protests "This is an outrage on the Press," James retorts: "Then it'll wipe out one by the Press on the Public—an' leave just a million over."

As *The Foundations* was produced in 1917, the author was clearly at no pains to conceal his opinion of the Press even while the war was raging. *Saint's Progress*, written in 1917-1918, was not published until 1919, but although the War was over, the war spirit was by no means banished from the land and it still needed some moral courage to venture to criticise either the Government or any of the institutions by which the Government was upheld, Army, Navy, Church, or Press. *Saint's Progress* reveals, more than any other of Galsworthy's novels, the state of his mind during the progress of the War, and his views on the Press are not disguised. No newspaper came on Sunday to the country town of Kestrel where the Reverend Edward Pierson was staying, not even the local paper, which had so long and so nobly done its bit with head-lines to win the war. No news whatever came, of men blown up, to enliven the hush of that hot June afternoon. "What humbugs we are!" thought Fort. "To read the newspapers and the speeches you'd believe everybody thought of nothing but how to get killed for the sake of the future. Drunk on verbiage!" And the Editor in *The Burning Spear*, not to mention the news editor Mr. Crackamup, admittedly farcical characters, are further evidence of Galsworthy's disinclination to grant any virtue to the Press in War-time.

This almost excessive bitterness is undoubtedly explained by the intensity of his feelings. War was a crime, he felt, and whoever contributed to its prolongation or insincerely glorified it, shared in the offence. Bitterness is a frequent enough phenomenon in Galsworthy's work, but cynicism is almost completely absent. Cynicism, when it does not camouflage sentimentality—and sometimes when it does— betrays a fundamental disbelief in life: the only logical outcome of cynicism is suicide. But bitterness, because it is the result of disappointment and is a recognition that events have gone awry, confesses to a belief in a right course, and, by deduction, in ultimate perfection. If Galsworthy had not believed, with Courtier (*The Patrician*) that the world was ruled by love, and not by power and the fear which power produces, he would not have been so bitter in the presence of forces which retarded the attainment of the ultimate goal. To assist, as the Press in war-time did, the increase of the sum of hatred in a world of which the mainspring should be love, was the cardinal offence, the unforgivable sin against the Holy Spirit. It showed a cynical disregard of the Truth which makes men free and an absence of that social conscience which ought to be the most treasured possession of every public man.

"A TERRIBLE AND FIERCE THING"

"A TERRIBLE AND FIERCE THING"

"CONSCIENCE, in Miltoun, was a terrible and fierce thing." (*The Patrician*). For "Miltoun" read, in this connection, "Galsworthy." From the time when his earliest hero set forth, armed with pen and tongue and no more deadly weapon, to wage war upon the Philistines and expose the hypocrisy of the Pharisees, Galsworthy was a fighter whose only Lord was a peculiarly sensitive conscience. In the lesser realms of behaviour he was not unconventional: he wore the clothes which would have made a less conspicuous man unconspicuous and conformed in manners to the standards of his class and age. But in fundamentals—religion, the deeper relations between man and man, the duty of man in relation to the world and the universe, he went his own way, not flouting convention, for Galsworthy could never have been appropriately called a flouter, but ignoring convention if it conflicted with his conscience.

> Come! Let us lay a crazy lance in rest,
> And tilt at windmills under a wild sky!
> For who would live so petty and unblest
> That dare not tilt at something ere he die,
> Rather than, screened by safe majority,
> Preserve his little life to little ends,
> And never raise a rebel battle cry!

Notwithstanding this invitation, however, rebel-

lion would be too violent a word to apply to the
customary Galsworthy approach. Many a time I
have been with him when turbulent spirits, by the
violence of conviction which brooked no criticism,
have threatened to destroy the very instrument which
might achieve the result they wished, and have seen
how, sharing their opinions but seeing beyond them
to the possibility of equally sincere if mistaken alter-
natives, he has won a victory for tolerance. Fight,
yes, but choose fair weapons, believe in the cause
for which you fight, make sure that the other fellow
has a fair deal, and expect no reward. That was his
creed.

> So! Undismayed beneath the serried clouds
> Shall float the banner of forlorn defence—
> A jest to the complacency of crowds—
> But haloed with the one diviner sense:
> To hold itself as nothing to itself;
> And in the quest of the imagined star
> To lose all thought of after-recompense!

Galsworthy waged war with a dozen social evils,
and some of his battles are recorded in these pages,
but more than anything else, he waged war upon
war. It is doubtful if he ever believed in war; it is
certain that as he grew older his abhorrence of war
grew deeper, and he gave a considerable part of his
time to combating it. His hatred of cruelty, his intense delight in physical beauty, all his instincts sup-
ported his reasoned conviction that war was futile,
unnecessary and an abomination; for every problem
it solved it created a dozen others, for every account
it squared, it opened a hundred more. "War," he
wrote in an open letter to the Disarmament Conference in 1932, "however you look at it, is an insensate

folly. It achieves no real end; no sane or lasting satisfaction for national honour; no true economic benefit; not even a strengthening of fibre through suffering and effort, for though it may be a purge at first, it becomes a wasting disease long before its close."

Certainly not unaware of the glamour of warfare to certain types of mind, nor of the frequent heroism of soldiers, it is significant that there are no battle scenes in all Galsworthy's many pages and no soldier-hero who is not a soldier in spite of himself. For army men as individuals he has occasionally shown a certain indulgence. There is, for instance, Dinny's father, General Charwell, who first appears in *Maid in Waiting*, a sympathetic character who is not, however, shown in a military setting or in circumstances which much reveal his soldier's mentality. Soldiers and the army, in the few places where Galsworthy refers to them, are held up to mild, unmalicious derision. I remember old General Pendyce, waiting in the hall of the Stoics Club; a somewhat pathetic character, whose back had that look about it of a man whose occupation has been taken from him. And while he waited he tried as far as possible to think of nothing. Having served his country, his time now was nearly all devoted to waiting, and to think fatigued and made him feel discontented, for he had had sunstroke once and fever several times. In the perfect precision of his collar, his boots, his dress, his figure; in the way from time to time he cleared his throat, in the strange yellow whiskers, in the immobility of his white hands on his cane, he gave the impression of a man sucked dry by a system. (*Country House*.) Mr. Pogram, who will be remembered for the odour of lavender and gutta-percha which he exhaled, thought that the wild young things of to-day were better in the army—safe in the army. No ideas there! (*Freelands*.)

"*THE RESTLESS CREEPING OF THE TIGER SPIRIT*" . . .

The Great War is celebrated by Galsworthy in many places, incidentally and directly I have always assumed that *The Skin Game*, with which he leaped to popular appreciation in 1920, was in some sort an allegory of the War. Symbolism he almost habitually eschewed, but there are certainly a number of instances where symbolism of a kind was employed by him, and in *The Skin Game* the situation is worked out in such a way that frequently it runs parallel with the situation of the War. The combatants start off with the full conviction that they are severally in the right. Land-owning, die-hard, self-satisfied, refined Hillcrist; vulgar, pushing, honest, rapacious Hornblower—each of them imagines that his own point of view is the only point of view, that his conduct is the only possible conduct. Hillcrist would preserve the amenities and dignities of English tradition; Hornblower would develop the industrial possibilities of the country. The standpoints are not incompatible save where the carrying-out of the one impinges on the privileges of the other. Hornblower would have been applauded if he had confined his activities to areas which had already been debased by industrialism: his crime was in wishing to develop a piece of land by building a factory on it in the direct line of vision of the Hillcrist country seat. The conflict is precipitated by Hornblower turning out of their homes some humble cottagers named Jackman who had formerly been on the Hillcrist estate but had become the Hornblowers' tenants

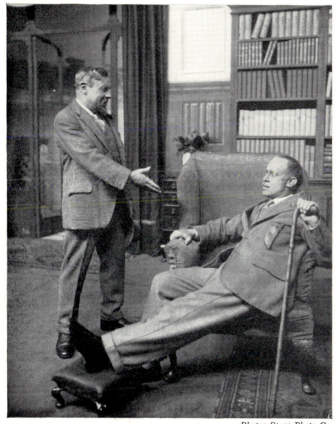

Photo: Stege Photo Co.

A SCENE FROM " THE SKIN GAME."
NICHOLAS HANNEN as " Gilchrist "; EDMUND GWENN as " Hornblower."

To face p. 58.

owing to the sale of a piece of land. As the battle continues, and one weapon is added to another, each dirtier than the last, the Jackmans are completely forgotten until a few minutes before the final curtain, when they return to thank Hillcrist for having saved them from eviction; they retire, finding no welcome, and Hillcrist says with bitter but unconscious irony: "I'd forgotten their existence." It is impossible not to identify the Jackmans with those "smaller nationalities" in defence of whose rights the Great War was waged.

The points of similarity between the Great War and the "skin game" played by the Hillcrists and the Hornblowers are inescapable, but the parallel is not unnaturally stressed, and it would be inadmissible to identify any of the belligerents with the dramatis personæ. It is quarrelling itself that is pilloried—not one antagonist rather than another. "One can't fight and not grow bitter," says Jill. With the growth of a quarrel there grows a myopic condition which renders the opponents' legitimate claims invisible. Jill, the younger generation, is dragged into the quarrel unwillingly and has fewer illusions than the others. "There isn't any big point of view," she declares cynically; "we're all out for our own." The quarrel well under way, it is not human to measure consequences. And Hillcrist's question: "Who knows where things end when they once begin?" is more legitimately, perhaps, the author's wonder than his own. "What is it that gets loose when you begin a fight, and makes you what you think you're not? What blinding evil? Begin as you may, it ends in this—skin game . . . When we began this fight, we had clean hands—are they clean now? What's gentility worth if it can't stand fire?"

As pointing the same moral, it is relevant to recall the quarrel in *The Silver Spoon*, with Fleur Mont and Marjorie Farrars as antagonists. Beginning with a relatively trivial incident, such as would have passed unremarked if Soames had not become touchy, it leads to endless bad feeling, humiliation, recriminations, the stirring of a cesspool which contaminates all who come near it. Awakened to the knowledge that he must now set about raking up all he could against the Farrars woman, Soames decided that society law-suits were like the war: you might win and regret it ever afterwards, or lose and regret it more.

Soldiers on active service came little into the Galsworthy field; but his strictures on war certainly do not include a ban on them. Indeed, they are generally held to be the victims of politicians at home, and of course of the Press who through blindness or cupidity urge the wilder claims of false patriotism. "I wish to God I were back in France," said Fort (*Saint's Progress*). "One doesn't feel clean here!" And Bob Pierson, thinking of the men at the Front, felt as if the top of his head would come off. "And those politician chaps spouting away in every country—how they can have the cheek!" It was a soldier, wounded and back from France, too, who cried: "The war! The cursed war! In the unending rows of little grey houses, in huge caravanserais and the mansions of the great, in villas, and huge slum tenements; in the government offices, and factories, and railway stations where they worked all night; in the long hospitals where they lay in rows; in the camp prisons of the interned; in barracks, workhouses, palaces—no head, sleeping or waking," so imagined this soldier, "would be free of that thought:

'The cursed war!'" And then he is held up by the sight of a church spire, rising ghostly over the roofs, and ponders that churches alone, void of the human soul, would be unconscious. "If Christ were real," he mused, "He'd reach that moon down and go chalking 'Peace' with it on every door of every house, all over Europe. But Christ's not real, and Hindenburg and Harmsworth are."

This thought, that a Christian Church had no role in a world at war unless it were to combat the war spirit and rally to the call of the Prince of Peace, was recurrent. It is not by chance that he makes his Dean in *The Mob*— produced in March 1914— bolster up the State against the pacifist Stephen More who claims the right to follow his conscience. "The Government is dealing here with a wild lawless race, on whom I must say I think sentiment is rather wasted," says the Dean. "We have the right to chastise." And forgetting that he represents One who declared that father and mother, sister and brother, must if necessary be denied in order that a man should follow his own vision, he claims that there comes a point where the individual conscience must resign itself to the country's feeling.

Of how much finer calibre is the Reverend Edward Pierson in *Saint's Progress*, who at least is faintly aware of the incongruity of his situation as a minister of Christ at a time when the precepts of Christ were treasonable. Struggling to see straight in another matter affecting his ministry, he came again to that perpetual gnawing sense which had possessed him ever since the war began, that it was his duty to be dead. To be a Christian as Tolstoy understood the word—and no one else in our time has had logic and love of truth enough to give it coherent meaning—is (to be quite sincere) not suited to men of Western blood, wrote Galsworthy on another occasion. And the word in this passage which needs more than the emphasis of parentheses is "sincere." Our special besetting sin, of wishing to have our cake and to eat it too, was certainly not quiescent in war-time. We loved to raise the flag of liberty and muster beneath its shade all who did or did not believe in our inevitable rightness. Mr. Lavender's speech in the market-place went but a trifle beyond the bounds of verisimilitude: "Only by preserving the freedom of individual conscience, and at the same time surrendering it whole-heartedly to every call which the State makes on us, can we hope to defeat the machination of the arch-enemies of mankind." (*Burning Spear.*)

It is not perhaps surprising that Galsworthy's only humorous book—*The Burning Spear*—should have been a satirical attack on war. So deeply did he feel the war that it was only possible to write of it at length if he were able to maintain a certain detachment—and this a satirical vehicle enabled him to do. *The Burning Spear*, written in 1918, was published under a pen-name in 1919. In 1918, he wrote a short essay, a postscript to the misery of the war period, entitled "A Green hill far away", and in this, without the crust of satire, we glimpse something of what he had suffered during the period when at every tick of his watch some human body was being mangled or destroyed. "Now it is December; an armistice has been declared. Peace! It is still incredible," he writes. "No more to hear with the ears of the nerves the ceaseless roll of gunfire, or see with the eyes of the nerves drowning men, gaping wounds, and death. . . . Each day this thought of peace becomes more real and blessed. I can lie on this green hill and praise Creation that I am alive in a world of beauty. I can go to sleep up here with the coverlet of sunlight warm on my body, and not wake to that old dull misery." He revels in the beauty of the earth, and gazes at a far gleam of sea, knowing that there is no murk of murder on it any more. And he thinks how of all the countless millions who have fought and nursed and written and spoken and dug and sewn and worked in a thousand other ways to help on the business of killing, hardly any have laboured in real love of war . . . "Can wars, then, ever cease?" he asks. "Look in men's faces, read their writings, and beneath masks and hypocrisies note the restless creeping of the tiger spirit. There has never been anything to prevent the millenium except the nature of the human being." And back he comes to his old cry, implicit in all his work, the theme *par excellence* of the Forsyte chronicles. "There are not enough lovers of beauty among men. It all comes back to that."

I did not know Galsworthy during the war, and as it has not been my practice in this book to lay much stress on hearsay, I shall only briefly refer to the part he played in the war. During the first few years, up to the middle of 1916, he produced a great deal of work which was sold chiefly in America and brought in money for English relief funds. Then he trained for hospital work and obtained a certificate for Swedish massage, of which he had already had some experience, and he went, with his wife as secretary and *lingère*, to a Benevole hospital at Martouret, Die, Drôme, under the auspices of the Franco-British Red Cross—for which service, by the way, both he and

Mrs. Galsworthy received decorations. That was from November 1916 to March 1917. On his return, he became one of the chief appeal-writers, if not the chief, for war relief funds; and all the time he was giving time, work, money, strength, a motor ambulance, saddles, and manuscripts. In 1918 he was, I am told, "up for service," but was turned down, not only because he was over age, but on account of his eyesight and a groggy shoulder.

Mr. Edward Fuller of the Save the Children Fund tells me that he approached Galsworthy in 1919 and invited him to write an article drawing attention to the acute suffering of children in Central Europe. With characteristic honesty, he replied that not having visited the areas affected since the war, he did not feel able to do what was asked. "But he did not limit himself to a point-blank refusal," says Mr. Fuller: "with his letter he enclosed a personal gift of £100 (the first of many generous subscriptions) and some lines which he intimated could be used without reserve in the cause of the work. These lines were published in 'The Daily News' and subsequently in various other papers. Not only did this touch many hearts and bring a substantial amount of contributions to the Save the Children Fund, but the manuscript was subsequently sold on behalf of the Save the Children Fund." Galsworthy retained an interest in the work of the Save the Children Fund till his death, and his pen and purse were both liberally used in its service.

"FROM HAND TO MOUTH" . . .

The war over, Galsworthy, like the rest of us, dreamed dreams of reconstruction; there came a revival of faith in humanity and a tempered belief

in the possibility of warding off future wars. For
some years the ravages of war, the healing of nations,
the re-establishment of human contacts severed by
the war, occupied the minds of men of goodwill and
Galsworthy did not fail to take his part in this necessary service. The first novel that followed the Armistice and continued the Forsyte Saga—*In Chancery*—
covered a period so much earlier than that of the
Great War that even elliptical reference to it would
probably have thrown the whole structure out of
gear—a risk which Galsworthy, careful artist that he
was, could be trusted to avoid. The South African
war comes into it, and Jolyon's doubts as to its wisdom and righteousness might conceivably, but im-
probably, be translated into an indirect reference to
the European conflict. Even *To Let*, published in
1921, steers clear of any but the most casual of
references to the war. Jack Cardigan, we learn, kept
fit during the war period in order to kill Germans;
and young Michael Mont declares that the great dis-
covery of the War is that we all thought we were pro-
gressing—now we know we're only changing. And
when old Timothy Forsyte came to die, that one-
pure individualist left in a world diluted by the en-
croachments of co-operation, he was unique also as
the only man who hadn't heard of the Great War.

Subsequently, as if in repentance of having left so
colossal a formative influence out of the scheme of his
work, Galsworthy wrote *Soames and the Flag*, drawing
together the impressions of four years and four
months and revealing them through the mind of a
Soames grown mellower and less predatory, but not
less secretive and reticent, scarcely less hard-headed,
but moved, like all but the most cynically detached,
by the subtle instinct of patriotism. *Soames and the*

5

Flag is not a story; it has no form save the form which any narrative starting with the outbreak of war and closing with the declaration of the Armistice would automatically assume: it is the statement of a point of view—Soames' point of view, but not necessarily always at variance with Galsworthy's. We find certain points of unmistakable identity. War is declared. And now all over Europe they were going to blow each other to bits. What would the parsons say? Nothing—he shouldn't wonder—they were a funny lot. An opinion not remote from Galsworthy's own, as we have seen. And as the war progressed, with advances and set-backs, because, forsooth, nothing could stop it once it had got going, Soames looked on, a lonely sharer in the disaster, denied the relief of confidence and sympathy because he was not made that way. He was privileged to see a Zeppelin burst into flames, but like Pierson in *Saint's Progress*, he had imagination enough to realise that the crew, however perfidious, were being burned alive, and the knowledge gave him no satisfaction. The hysteria, the night-clubs and the made-up faces—all these phenomena of the war struck him as un-English and therefore to be deprecated; no less un-English was the bullying of conscientious objectors, with whose conscience he had no sympathy, however; and, indeed, conscription itself was as un-English as anything else, interfering with the sanctity of private feelings. If he had been forty instead of sixty he would presumably have joined up, but the mere notion gave him a pain below the ribs, so crude, so brutal and so empty did all this military business appear to him. In spite of everything, the war did come to an end. No more sudden death, no more bombs, no more drowning ships, no more young devils taken from home and killed! And Soames stood in St. Paul's cathedral whither he had gone because it was big and old and empty, and English; and on his restrained pale face upturned was a look wistful and sardonic. . . .

Is it being super-subtle to relate the "look wistful" to the sad and sorry past and the "look sardonic" to the ambiguous future, which Soames, not without a gift of deductive prophesy, darkly glimpsed? Certain it is that treaties and industrial pacts, leagues and a multitude of well-intentioned groups, failed to remove the doubts and fears which the war—the joy-bells of peace having been suitably rung—left by way of heritage; and Galsworthy's last six novels, completing the Forsyte chronicles and ramifying into the Charwells, faithfully reflect this period of disillusion, scepticism, cynicism and idealistic groping. Wilfrid Desert was too individual to be typical of the younger generation that went through the war, but a good many of them would have shared his state of mind if they had been permitted to know it. "I lived so long with horror and death; I saw men so in the raw; I put hope of anything out of my mind so utterly, that I can never more have the faintest respect for theories, promises, conventions, moralities and principles. I have hated too much the men who wallowed in them while I was wallowing in mud and blood. Illusion is off. No religion and no philosophy will satisfy me—words, all words . . . I am dangerous, but not so dangerous as those who trade in words, principles, theories, and all manner of fanatical idiocy to be worked out in the blood and sweat of other men. The war's done one thing for me—converted life to comedy. Laugh at it there's nothing else to do!"

JOHN GALSWORTHY

The utterance is extreme, as Wilfrid was extreme—
and it was never given mouth to; but it expresses
with reasonable fidelity the harshness produced in
many young men who, born to high ideals of service,
found themselves frustrated by the War, their finer
feelings inhibited and their most individual qualities
suppressed by the necessity to conform to a pattern
imposed from without. Such men were fated either
to go under in a sea of cynicism, or like Wilfrid, find a
modified salvation in a life of action, with the prospect
of visitations from the ghosts of suppressed desires.

A commoner attitude was that of the realist Fleur,
true daughter of her French mother. "Life! Oh!
well, we know it's supposed to be a riddle, but we've
given it up. We just want to have a good time
because we don't believe anything can last. But I
don't think we know how to have it . . . I like seeing
everything that's new and worth while, or seems so
at the moment. But that's just how it is—nothing
lasts . . . I don't believe in anyone or anything—
much." Even Mr. Blythe, holding forth in "The
Outlook" office, opined that we needed fifty settled
years to reach the *status quo ante bellum* and knew that
we were not likely to get them. "We've struck a disturbed patch of history, and we know it in our bones,
and live from hand to mouth, according." And old
Soames, coming as it were out of a trance, once pronounced that the war had left everything unsettled.
"I suppose people believe in something nowadays,
but *I* don't know what it is." Responding to his
earnest young son-in-law Michael's probing into the
nature of his own beliefs, he expanded: "They
expect too much now; there's no interest taken in
being alive"—the possible answer, thought Michael,
to all modern doubt.

But merely to observe the symptoms of the disease which afflicted post-war society was not enough; a diagnosis was necessary before a cure could even be sought, and the later books of Galsworthy, in the incidental way which was peculiarly his method, do, at any rate, hint at the nature of the disease. Into the winning of the war (by whichever side) was poured not only a good deal of meanness and self-interest,but a vast quantity of idealism, disinterested fervour, self-sacrifice and courage. Discounting the mercenaries and those to whom a fight, for any cause or none, is a joy in itself, and those to whom the war was an escape from the intolerable dullness of their lives or the difficulties of domesticity, there were still many millions of young and middle-aged men who gave up their private lives with their civilian clothes and surrendered themselves to a controlling power which they honestly believed subserved some high ideal: whether they called the ideal England or Germany, France or Russia, Serbia or Bulgaria; whether they believed that they were fighting a war to end war, or were protecting their civilisation or their territory from the onslaughts of marauders, is beside the point. They were animated by motives that were relatively pure and the attainment of their goal was expected to synchronise, if not with the millenium, at least with the beginning of a new social order in which lands-fit-for-heroes-to-live-in might be taken for granted and world disarmament as a matter of course. That the belief was a naïve one makes it the more pathetically admirable: it was, after all, a belief upon which governments banked and which professional propagandists exploited. The explosion of the belief within a few months of the Armistice did more than destroy the immediate illusions: it made it difficult for the disillusioned to hold any beliefs at all. Not only faith was shattered, but hope. Existence, moral and physical, was hand to mouth and the future too murky to be pondered, or, if pondered, pondered with pessimism.

This, it seems to me, is a fair diagnosis of the post-war symptoms and is implicit in Galsworthy's later novels. Old Sir Lawrence Mont, challenged, utters his warning: "I should be glad to think that men really believed in humanity, and all that, but you know they don't—they believe in novelty and getting their own way. With rare exceptions they're still monkeys, especially the scientific variety; and when you put gunpowder and a lighted match into the paws of monkeys, they blow themselves up to see the fun. Monkeys are only safe when deprived of means to be otherwise . . ." and much more to the same enlivening purpose, winding up with "I hope I'm wrong. But we're driving fast to a condition of things when millions can be killed by the pressing of a few buttons. What reason is there to suppose that our bumps of benevolence will increase in time to stop our using these great new toys of destruction?"

Ten years have passed since that was written. Is it less apt to-day than then? The threat of war, remote or near, resided in Galsworthy's consciousness and in none of his books is it entirely ignored. Not dragged in like King Charles's head, it comes as a necessary part of the psychological atmosphere of the world he is depicting. Who would have children, thinks Michael Mont, for the mere pleasure of seeing them blown up, poisoned, starved to death? A few fanatics would hold on, the rest of the world go barren. This in 1922. A couple of years later Michael is still wondering whether progress has been found out.

Poison gas and town blight hang over our heads, he says; and round about the same period a young Under-Secretary vouched for the fact that he knew a fellow who had got a ray that would go through three bullocks, a nine-inch brick wall, and give a shock to a donkey on the other side, and that only at quarter strength. The American Hallorsen (*Maid in Waiting*), less facetious, is not less convinced that the progress of science was heading us for hell. If France and Italy came to blows there'd be no Rome, no Paris, no Florence, no Venice, no Lyons, no Milan, no Marseilles within a fortnight. They would be poisoned deserts. Even Hilary, most human of all Galsworthy's parsons, waxes sarcastic in the face of the imminence of more efficient scientific war-fare. "Now that flying and poison gas have made food for powder unnecessary, and unemployment is rampant," he said, "I'm afraid there's no question but that it's unpatriotic *not* to believe in limiting our population. As for our Christian principles; being patriots, we didn't apply the Christian principle 'Thou shalt not kill' during the war; so, being patriots, we can't logically apply the Christian principle 'Thou shalt not limit' now."

"*THE FLOWERING OF THE ALOE . . .*"

In citing passages like the above I do not wish it to be inferred that Galsworthy, having decided that another world war was inevitable, folded his hands and sat waiting for the grim prophecy to be made good. Warning, in any case, rather than prophecy would be the right word to apply to his utterances, and far from acquiescing in the horrors which his imagination called up, he devoted much time and energy, not to mention money, to ensuring that they should never be permitted to take place. Particularly did he plead the cause of the children. "When a child is outraged or done to death in time of peace," he wrote in that letter to the Disarmament Conference from which I have already quoted, "the whole nation is stirred. In war time, millions of children are outraged and done to death, in manners not the same, but as horrible. On them are forced slow starvation, illness, deformities, orphanage, death from disease, gas and bombs. From them is rived all fatherly control, so that in many cases they become little criminals. Under-nourished and stunted physically and morally, they are taken from school prematurely and set to war work. The effects of war are felt by them for years after war is over, often for the rest of their lives. Fortunate are those hundreds of thousands who, but for war, would have been born and are not . . . Let those men who will meet soon now, for the avowed purpose of considering how far they can minimize the chances and the scope of war, put, each one to himself, this question: If I were incited to outrage and murder a child, what should I say and do to him who incited me? And let them remember that, however far from their thoughts it be that children should suffer, War will inevitably outrage and destroy them. Verily, the health, moral welfare, and lives of millions of children, generation by generation, depend on how far they shall succeed in their coming efforts to rescue the future from the headstrong follies of the present, and the bitter cruelties, wastage and degradations of the past."

This appeal was addressed to the delegates to the Conference for the reduction and limitation of Armaments which was held in Geneva in 1932.

Galsworthy had a loyal belief, tempered by a

certain scepticism of the machinery, in the idea and the ideals of the League of Nations, which Sir Lawrence Mont, by the way, regarded as about the only sensible product of our time and hoped to live to see America embrace an institution founded by an American; a hope which, in Galsworthy's case, was left unfulfilled.

Of all the forces against international strife with which Galsworthy associated himself after the war, the P.E.N. engaged most of his attention. The P.E.N. is an international association of writers (*P*laywrights, *P*oets, *E*ditors, *E*ssayists and *N*ovelists) founded in 1921 by the novelist and poet Mrs. C. A. Dawson Scott. Its object is to promote friendliness and hospitality among writers throughout the world irrespective of nationality, race or creed, and by this means help to bring about that understanding which, if achieved, would insure amity among nations. The potential influence of authors united on a basis of this kind cannot be gainsaid, and the annual international congresses which have already been held in London, New York, Paris, Berlin, Brussels, Vienna, Oslo, Warsaw, The Hague, Budapest, and Dubrovnik have testified to the pregnancy of the idea. In spite of the economic stress which has prevailed during the greater part of the P.E.N.'s adolescence, the association shows no signs of dwindling strength. Fifty centres in thirty-five countries, with a total membership of more than four thousand—that is its statistical strength. Galsworthy was one of the first writers whom Mrs. Dawson Scott infected with the germ of the idea and he welcomed it with enthusiasm. It was his suggestion that she should arrange a dinner at which writers could be acquainted with the scheme and their co-operation be invited; and when she, following his advice with that docility typical of her, arranged the function and asked him to attend, he wrote to her as follows:

"Anything which promotes the internationality of art is good. The material and roots of art are essentially national, or shall we say individual and local; but when once a work of art is achieved, all national and local barriers should be let down."

THE P.E.N.

He came to the dinner and was asked to be the first President of the P.E.N. He declined. He was asked again, the instrument of Mrs. Dawson Scott's enthusiasm being Mr. C. S. Evans, who had just launched the first "omnibus" edition of *The Forsyte Saga*, and at the second time of asking he succumbed. He was President of the London P.E.N. till his death, when the robes of office were assumed by Mr. H. G. Wells. Galsworthy's most vital contribution during these early days to the P.E.N. was the suggestion that there should be an international congress once a year, designed to bring writers together in the flesh, and when the first congress was held, in London, he worked unceasingly to make it a success.

It was at the inaugural dinner of the P.E.N. in October 1921 at the Florence Restaurant that I saw Galsworthy for the first time. I do not remember whether I was introduced to him. I can only conjure up a vision of an austere, courtly English gentleman, in appearance more like an ideal lawyer than an artist, whose hair was already grey though he was some years off sixty, and whose nobly domed head and steady steel-blue eyes did not encourage familiarity. I gained an impression then, later deepened and subsequently obliterated, that he was aloof, unapproachable, unbending. He was none of these things. He was shy, and for one so travelled and accustomed to ceremonies, peculiarly retiring, and his *sang froid*, I afterwards discovered, was quite fictitious. But it was not until 1924 that I really became acquainted with him, when I was elected to the Executive Committee of the P.E.N. and found myself seated next to him, on trial, at the dinner which synchronised with the annual general meeting. The nervousness of a newcomer was soon dispelled, partly perhaps by the champagne provided by an ever-generous host, but chiefly by the charm of his gracious manners. I remember that we talked about modern art, with which he was not greatly in sympathy, and he was mildly amazed to find that I really liked, with reservations, the bird sanctuary in Kensington Gardens which had recently been erected as a memorial to his friend W. H. Hudson. Epstein's conception of Rima seemed to him gauche, ungracious, unbeautiful—infinitely remote from Hudson's; and he who rarely sided with mob opinion, was inclined to think that there was some justification for the outcry with which the memorial had been received, though none for the manner in which it had been expressed. The ten years which followed did not modify his opinion of the Rima carving; in his last book, when Dinny wished to make a rendezvous with Corven, she selected the Rima, in preference to the Achilles, saying "We can walk away from it."

During those ten years I saw a great deal of Galsworthy and had many opportunities of becoming acquainted with his feelings on such subjects as internationalism, nationalism, patriotism, war, peace, and the like. We had many talks, exchanged letters, met at innumerable committee meetings and went hand in hand to international congresses. If, therefore, I attribute to him opinions and attitudes for which there is no written warranty the validity of my conclusions need not be questioned. Working with him as closely as I did, I came to know what course of action he would be likely to take in given circumstances, and was often able to act for him without troubling him to make a decision. The President of an association like the P.E.N., with branches radiating over the five continents, is not likely to be left in splendid isolation by its four thousand members. Galsworthy's kind heart would not have been proof against the numerous unwarranted calls upon his time from which it was the duty of a secretary to protect him. Whether as a result of the interaction of opinion and opinion, or through the influence of one point of view on another, or on account of some fundamental similarity, there is no doubt that for many years I had no difficulty in identifying myself with Galsworthy's frame of mind and making decisions and expressing opinions of which I knew he would approve. That the decisions accorded with my own sense of fitness and the opinions tallied in most cases with mine, were happy accidents. Far be it from me to claim a particle of Galsworthy's astuteness in conducting committee meetings, or a fraction of his sagacity in so ordering events that a desired result might be achieved: my only claim is that, had I had his sagacity and astuteness, I should have employed them to similar ends.

Galsworthy's presidency of the P.E.N. was in no sense a sinecure. He disapproved of lending his name to any work in which he was not prepared to take an active share, and in the P.E.N. his share was an inestimable one. Not only did he fertilise the association with ideas, attend committees, dinners, congresses; draft appeals and resolutions: he would also give hours to tedious necessary trifles like addressing envelopes, folding circulars, and similar office-boy's tasks, with a readiness and lack of condescension which revealed his true modesty.

He was anxious that the P.E.N. should not claim too much. High-flown schemes, he knew, were apt to fizzle out quickly and discreditably. The P.E.N. should go slowly, modestly, having a carefully defined policy, and limit its scope to that until its power increased. The P.E.N. should provide a vehicle through which a certain floating, unmoored friendliness might manifest itself. "If the P.E.N. idea," he said on one occasion, "is looked on as a panacea for all evils, or even as a powerful preventive of international trouble, it is bound to disappoint and to furnish one more vanished illusion to a disillusioned world. Writers have no great, at least no direct influence on world affairs. Such influences as they exert are vague, and, as it were subterranean; and they do well not to pretend to possess political power they have not." On another occasion he wrote: "We writers have a real mission of goodwill to fulfil in the world; and there is no section of mankind better qualified to fulfil it, since the influence of friendliness between writers of many countries is subtle and far-reaching, and there is no end to its extension."

The principles which have governed the P.E.N. from the beginning might be expressed as follows:

(a) The promotion of international understanding through personal friendliness and hospitality among writers all over the world.

(b) A belief that nationality in art does not conflict with a belief in the right of untrammelled international circulation of art.

(c) Politics, the concern of the individual, should be left out of the activities of the P.E.N.

(d) It is the duty of members of the P.E.N. to use their influence in favour of good understanding and mutual respect between the nations, particularly in time of war.

I have a note of a speech which Galsworthy made many years ago—alas! it is undated and I cannot trace its immediate cause. He claimed that the P.E.N. could and "should be a sort of guardian to Literature and its cousins—Music, Painting and Sculpture against chauvinistic and sectional demons. It should attempt to guarantee such breadth of mind towards Art generally as should render impossible in the future spiteful and muddy-minded ostracism of this or that nation's art in times of conflict. In other words, the P.E.N. can educate the public opinion of the world to regard the achievements of art as supra-national, belonging to human nature as a whole, and supplying wants intellectual and emotional, which have nothing to do with material strife between nations. The dispensation of hospitality comes next in importance. It is not a question of food and drink but of the occasions they furnish for the rubbing of French shoulders with German shoulders, English noses with Hungarian, Russian, what-not. There is much lugubrious truth in the old saying: 'Here's a stranger; heave half a brick at him!' Nothing is more appalling in this world than the prejudice excited by ignorance; when fomented by the unscrupulous 'patriot' it is the stuff of conflagration. If the P.E.N. can bring to the writers of the world, including the Press, a feel-

Bacon's Essays X

Gulliver

Vicar of Wakefield : She stoops to conquer :

Decline & Fall : If too long guiding autobiography

Boswell's Johnson

Amelia (Tom Jones being probably too well known)

Pride & Prejudice

Essays of Elia

East of Flaubourg (Robinson Crusoe etc)

Wuthering Heights

Vanity Fair (If translated then Barry Lyndon)

Adam Bede

Beauchamp's Career

Tess (Alternatively 'Far from the Madding Crowd')

Speke's Sources of the Nile

Macaulay's Essays.

Alice in Wonderland. & Through the the Looking Glass

Heroes & Hero Worship

Esther Waters

The Purple Land

Midshipman Easy (or if translated Peter Simple)

A TENTATIVE LIST OF BOOKS PUBLISHED BEFORE 1900 RECOMMENDED FOR TRANS-
LATION ; HAMMERED OUT AT A SELECT COMMITTEE OF THE P.E.N. AND NOTED BY
JOHN GALSWORTHY.

ing that to pervert the truth about an enemy is as
bad as to pervert it about a friend, it would have won
half the battle of Peace."

England was the back-ground, the atmosphere and
the inspiration of Galsworthy's work and in it he
rarely went beyond her coastline—two or three times
to Austria, for a brief spell to America, once to Hungary, once or twice to France; and even in those foreign
parts it is, with rare exceptions, English men and
English women who compose the dramatis personæ.
In spite of this absorption in his native land, he was
from early manhood a widely travelled man and he
was always at pains to understand foreigners and to
estimate national characteristics. He read French
with great ease, understood it when spoken and
spoke it diffidently but accurately. German he
understood less well, but I always had the impression
that he managed to get the sense of a speech in German if the orator had not been too eloquently im-
passioned, in which case he would turn to me with
that sudden smile of his and ask: "Was there anything in all that?" or "What was that all about?"
He had an unusual grasp of foreign affairs; had an
accurate impression of boundaries, and did not share
the average Englishman's delusion that Jugoslavia
and Czecho-Slovakia were one and the same. There
is ample evidence in his work of his awareness of
national characteristics. Sir Lawrence Mont had a
flair for classifying racial types, and Galsworthy
occasionally indulged him in it. His collection of
portraits (*Maid in Waiting*) revealed much shrewd-
ness. French culture is thus epitomised: Quick intelligence, wit, industry, decision, intellectual but
not emotional æstheticism, no humour, conventional

79

sentiment but no other, a having tendency . . . a
sense of form, no originality, very clear but limited
mental vision—nothing dreamy about her; quick
but controlled blood.

One might quarrel with some details of this sum-
ming-up, but in the main, how neat and accurate
this estimate is! The American woman, tip-top
culture variety, is evidently not so easily classifiable,
but Sir Lawrence has a shot at it. Notice chiefly,
he says, a look as if she had an invisible bit in her
mouth and knew it; in her eyes is a battery she'll
make use of but only with propriety. She'll be very
well preserved to the end of her days. Good taste, a
lot of knowledge, not much learning.—This docket-
ing of the American is less illuminating than many
other passages in Galsworthy's work in which
American and English are contrasted; but how
excellent this is of the German: Emotionally more
uncontrolled, and less sense of form than either of
those others, but has a conscience, is a hard worker,
great sense of duty, not much taste, some rather un-
handy humour . . . Plenty of sentiment, plenty of
good sound sense too!

And Dinny Charwell—taken as typical of the
English—is thus tabulated: Here we have a self-
consciousness, developed and controlled to the point
when it becomes unself-consciousness. To this lady
Self is the unforgivable intruder. We observe a
sense of humour, not devoid of wit, which informs
and somewhat sterilises all else. We are impressed
by what I may call a look not so much of domestic as
of public or social service, not to be found in our
other types. We discover a sort of transparency, as if
air and dew had got into the system. We decide that
*pre*cision is lacking, precision of learning, action,

thought, judgment, but that *de*cision is very present·
The senses are not highly developed; the æsthetic
emotions are excited more readily by natural than
by artificial objects. . . .

Both explicitly and implicitly, however, he has
many times bodied forth the Englishman, and may
be given credit for knowing as well as anybody of
what ingredients the pudding of English character,
as he called it, consisted. Italians, Belgians, Aus-
trians, Hungarians also come within his net, and
many instances of his concern for the difficulties of
some of the smaller nations have come to my knowledge. It was always his way to do good by stealth
and to dislike the fame which sometimes followed the
unexpected revelation of his generosity. I think it
was only after his death that it became known that
he had financed a soup kitchen in Budapest—only
one of many philanthropic ventures with which he
was associated. When the earthquake took place in
Bulgaria in 1928 he immediately wrote an appeal to
writers to fan the flame of sympathy for a little and
brave country which had met with so terrible a
misfortune.

"Earthquakes have wrecked hundreds of towns
and villages in the richest part of that country," he
wrote. "More than thirty-six thousand houses have
been wholly or partially destroyed; and two hundred
and sixty-five thousand people, most of them women,
children and old men, are without shelter. The
material loss is estimated at from two to four million
pounds, or more than one-third of the State Budget.
This crushing disaster has befallen a nation which
already had its back to the wall; a nation staggering
and over-burdened, whose lot has been heavy with
war, trouble and debt since 1912.

"The Bulgarians are respected by all for sterling qualities and indomitable courage; they are grimly facing the new calamity, desperate with the knowledge that out of their own resources they cannot hope to make good. Sympathy all must feel, but sympathy will not build houses, feed starving people, check the threatened epidemics. Of all men writers can best voice the universal sympathy for a brave and unfortunate nation, and stir that helpful sense of fellowship which lies in the hearts of modern men. I would, then, ask my fellow writers, who in so many countries follow the P.E.N. creed, to come with their eloquence to the rescue of the Bulgarian people in its dark hour."

I am glad to say that this appeal was not fruitless.

Mr. W. Rose Burns sent me a note about Galsworthy and Namaqualand which is worth quoting as typical of the remote ramifications of his kindliness. "O'okiep, in Namaqualand, once a flourishing copper city, with a club, polo team, cricket, football, and all the amenities, is now silent and deserted. The library of the derelict club was founded by the late John Galsworthy. A *Cape Argus* writer tells how the great writer visited the mining camp as a young man, an honoured guest, since his father was the solicitor of the Cape Copper Company. He found the miners without reading matter. When he returned to London he persuaded the directors to provide books for their men in the desert. He himself chose most of the books, and continued to do so as long as O'okiep demanded reading matter. But O'okiep died before John Galsworthy. *Fraternity* was the latest of his own works I could find among the books he had sent out. O'okiep in its palmiest days did not know its literary adviser as perhaps the leading man of English letters. When John Galsworthy died there were few copper miners left to mourn their lost patron. A fitter or two to mind the pumps; Frank Kitto and a couple of clerks; and old Jack Meadows, who can remember Galsworthy travelling on the narrow guage railway to Port Nolloth."

Galsworthy was in South Africa again in 1927 and while there endeavoured to found a centre of the P.E.N. It was not easy, for although the leading writers, like Sarah Gertrude Millin, the late Dorothea Fairbridge and others, were sympathetic enough to the idea, the great stretches of territory over which the score of writers were scattered made regular meetings difficult. However, in March, he heralded his partial success in a typically whimsical letter to me from Cape Town:

"I think I have succeeded in getting a skeleton centre started in S. Africa," he wrote; "or rather, two skeletons, one here and one at Johannesburg, co-equal and co-eternal, linked by what I hope will be the Holy Spirit."

If this were a history of the P.E.N. I should have a long tale to tell, touching on many matters and many people in many lands; but it is not. Here the P.E.N. is important only in so far as it reflects light on to Galsworthy. His prominence in the movement was so great that to ignore the part which it played in his life would be as distorting to a proper perspective as to over-emphasise it. My object will be to link together certain episodes and utterances which appear most significantly to reveal the man. The progress of the P.E.N. has been pointed by the international annual congresses, nearly all of which Galsworthy attended. He was not present at the second, in New York; but I have note of a message which he sent, containing some very Galsworthian words: "Friends—I use the word that should never be used without sincerity. . . . The flesh is three thousand miles away but the spirit is with you to-night." And he goes on to refer to "that kind and generous hospitality of America, which I have experienced so often, with a wonder amounting almost to consternation. I want to say to you that, whenever we companions of the P.E.N. meet, as you are meeting to-night, a wave of goodwill is released which brings its aroma to absent companions in lands far away. I beg you earnestly to believe that our meetings are not just festivity, but gestures of friendliness which have a deep and wide-reaching significance. The pen with the little *p* is mighty; the feelings of pen men and women are pervasive. What we feel to-day the world will feel to-morrow. In homely phrase: it is 'up to us' to make a better world of it. We are the voices. Our club exists to convert the wilderness."

It was in Paris, a year later, in 1924, that the P.E.N. was able to take a certain valuable initiative. Although the war had been over some years, the Treaty of Versailles continued to exert its influence as an irritant and between Germany and France feeling was scarcely less strained than it had been during the war. French troops were still in Germany; the Ruhr district still occupied. In spite of this, not only did the French P.E.N. centre send a particularly warm invitation to the Germans, but twenty-three writers accepted it with alacrity. It

"A TERRIBLE AND FIERCE THING"

was my first P.E.N. congress and I shall never forget
the atmosphere of cordiality in which Frenchmen
and Germans, for the first time since the war, strove
to obliterate the ill-feeling which had accumulated
during the previous ten years. The sight of the
P.E.N. thus performing the task of reconciliation
for which it had been founded was an enheartening
one to Galsworthy; but the next two congresses, in
Berlin and Brussels, were in some ways even more
impressive. Germany had been ostracised not only
during the war but for several years after the official
end of hostilities. Discounting any deliberate enmity,
the financial situation made international exchange
and intercourse difficult and often impossible. The
inflation of the Mark sent the prices of foreign books
up to fantastic heights which nobody but the richest
could afford to pay, and the newly rich in Germany
—war-profiteers and exchange-riggers—were not the
class that encouraged the love and spread of literature, native or foreign. "Brain hunger" was so great
that it almost amounted to mental starvation. If
foreign books and journals did not penetrate Germany, nor did foreign intellectuals, and the inflated
currency made it impossible for the cultured and
student classes in Germany to travel. The ostracism
had become automatic and not conscious, but its
effects were no less disastrous, and one was beginning
to wonder if Germany would ever regain a normal
footing in the comity of nations.

The initial attempt to break down the barriers
was made by the P.E.N., by deciding to hold a congress in Berlin. It was the first international congress of any kind to be held in Berlin since the Armistice and the moral effect was enormous. The efforts
made by national and civic authorities, as well as by

individuals, were stupendous. Relations severed by the war were rejoined; interrupted friendships were renewed, contacts of all kinds made. Galsworthy, already well known in Germany, was welcomed with enthusiasm, and with him representatives of a formidable list of the nations which had been against Germany in the Great War. "I swore that I would never go to Germany again, or meet a German in friendliness," said a young Serb to me, recalling the bombardment of Belgrade, "but here I am, and the language which you an Englishman, and I, a Serb, employ to understand each other is German."

Only one thing marred the universal friendliness, and that was not ill-feeling between the Germans and any members of other nationality, but between Germans and Germans, between the young and the not-so-young. I had noticed the absence of certain young authors whose work I knew, and made tentative inquiries. "We Germans are a quarrelsome people," said my informant with that pleasantly masochistic relish which is at least as common among Germans as the opposite tendency; and I learnt that a number of the youngest, more revolutionary, writers did not approve of the constitution of the German P.E.N. Centre: it was not, they said, representative of the best and most vital section of post-war German literature—they, in a word, were not members. I believe the German Press gave a certain amount of prominence to this cleavage, which was certainly unfortunate and incongruous. Some of the "young", unwilling that we should be misled, made representations to Galsworthy and to me and pleaded for a chance to state their case. It was then that Galsworthy assumed his not unfamiliar role of mediator. As I was personally acquainted with some of the "young", he charged me to invite them to lunch with him, and in due course we met at a little restaurant in a district which corresponds to Soho in London or Montmartre in Paris. Those whom I remember especially are Ernst Toller, since very well-known in England as the author of many plays including *Man and the Masses*, *Hinkeman*, *The Machine-wreckers*, and *Hoppla*; Arnolt Bronnen (I think, but would not vouch for it), the incredibly audacious young man who began as the most revolutionary of revolutionaries but has since, I gather, made a complete *volte face*; Herwarth Walden, sponsor of the *Stürm* movement, now abandoned and its sponsor in Russia; and Bert Brecht, a playwright who wrote several interesting plays in his early manhood and then turned to transforming English plays into German, so completely transforming them indeed that the originals would blush to be associated with them: The *Drei Groschen Oper* by Bert Brecht out of *The Beggar's Opera* is a famous example.

It was, considered in retrospect, an amusing occasion. Galsworthy spoke practically no German; mine was very much less good then, even, than it is now. Of the Germans only Toller spoke English at all, and he with no great ease—I remember how frequently he assured us that the situation was "penible", which indeed it was. Broken English and broken German, eked out with French, provided a sufficient means of communication, however, and before we separated, any ill-feeling there may have been was dissipated.

In no country were the post-war generation and their forebears so antagonistic as in Germany: the younger railed at their elders from platforms and in print, but rarely came face to face to rail in sight of each other. The executive members of the P.E.N. in Berlin had, apparently, remained aloof, and the younger writers, scorning the generation which "ran" the war, did not inquire into the qualifications of writers who had committed the sin of attaining middle-age. "Natürlich ist Herr Galsworthy was anderes," said one of them to me—"sehr sympatisch" and "reizend" and "garnicht pompös", said others— charm and understanding being considered outside the range of "arrived" German writers, and "pomposity" their peculiar prerogative. I can call up the picture of Galsworthy, lieutenanted by his wife, presiding with apparent ease over that luncheon table—one of a long series of meals at which he has played the host, for he had great faith in the humanising powers of food and drink.

The following year Brussels was the scene of the international meeting, and was made particularly significant by the fact that the delegates were welcomed on behalf of Belgium by that Burgomaster Max who had had a very different kind of task to perform when he had last received Germans on Belgian soil. M. Louis Piérard, author, critic, and member of the Belgian Chamber of Deputies, who organised the congress, writing to me recently, referred to Galsworthy in that multilingual manner typical of P.E.N. correspondence. "He was a great 'gentleman' of literature. He realised that mankind would go back to the darkest barbarism without an international reconciliation. In view of that necessary reconciliation, writers have a great mission to fulfil. I remember talking with him about those things during the Brussels conference, or in his Hampstead house. Ce fut un prince de l'intelligence

Front row, left to right: Louis Piérard, Georges Duhamel, John Galsworthy, Jules Romains, Mrs. Dawson Scott, Benjamin Crémieux.

P.E.N. Congress: Brussels, 1927.

To face p. 38

et une sorte de Balzac anglais de notre temps, un observateur de la société, au regard aigu." It was in Brussels, too, that from being a somewhat vague vehicle for the conveyance of friendliness and for making conciliatory gestures, the P.E.N., prompted by Galsworthy, adopted certain proposals, which he framed many months earlier, for making clear the principles for which the organisation came into being. These, if I may condense them, emphasised the importance of literature ignoring frontiers in spite of international upheavals, and pledged members to use their influence at all times in favour of good understanding and mutual respect between the nations.

At Brussels, again, Galsworthy was at pains to disassociate the P.E.N. from any belief in the possibility of destroying nationality, in life or literature; he believed profoundly in the importance of national traditions and would have had no sympathy with a movement whose aim was the levelling out of national characteristics by some process of mutual assimilation.

"Now that we of the P.E.N. clubs are meeting internationally for the fifth time," he said, "there is one thought I should like to try to put into words. It is this: Nationalism and Internationalism are not rivals; they are really complementary the one to the other. Those who wish prosperity to their own countries will be well advised to consider how in this twentieth century their countries can possibly gain or keep prosperity without the existence of international good will and consideration. I do not suppose there are any among us to-night who do not wish the best for their own countries; and if we differ at all from others it is only in that we see more clearly that the

best can only come in a world of nations which fore-
swear envy, malice, and all uncharitableness. Of
one thing we may be sure—national advantage
sought in an unscrupulous and purely selfish spirit
is no true national advantage.

"Monsieur le Président, I do not wholly despair of
a future wherein nations shall compete not for
territory and trade, but for repute; when to say: I
am a Belgian, a Frenchman, a German, a Swede,
may be to say: I am a citizen of the country that
hopes to render most service to mankind at large."

At Brussels, too, the question of censorship raised
its head for the first, but by no means for the last,
time. Galsworthy always fought shy of it, not because
he had any belief in censorship, but because the
question would, in almost every country, become a
political question, and the P.E.N. was pledged to
stand aside from politics. In England, except in war-
time, we associate the idea of censorship with the
Lord Chamberlain's Office and the banning of plays.
The battle of censorship here has been partly won.
In those days when Galsworthy among others raged
against the iniquitous banning of worthy works from
the privilege of stage performance, we cited with
ardent reiteration *Mrs. Warren's Profession*, *Waste*,
Monna Vanna, certain plays of Brieux, and possibly
Wilde's *Salome*, and we pointed scornfully at *The
Spring Chicken* or some such morsel which the Censor
permitted. To-day I for one should find it difficult
to name a play which the Lord Chamberlain is
forcibly preventing me from seeing. When, therefore, some apparently innocent member of the P.E.N.
abroad suggests that the international federation
should take a stand against censorship, the reaction
of the average English member is to applaud the

suggestion, believing it to have reference to the suppression of works of art on the grounds of some puritanical code of morality. What occasioned the suggested introduction of the subject in Brussels I cannot remember, but Galsworthy—whose astuteness could be trusted—was very anxious that it should not be raised. "In my view," he wrote to me, "any public discussion of such a matter is to be avoided like Satan himself in the interests of the Club. Everybody has got to realize that the good of the Club and its idea comes first and our private reluctances and dislikes second." And, in a later letter: "I think personally, that it's an impossible subject. Too many different customs and temperaments to arrive at any useful generalisation." I was not in the least surprised to find, when the matter came up for debate in Brussels, that the ground had been so carefully prepared that all danger of a political hornet's nest being disturbed was avoided. Georges Duhamel, most vivacious, slick and businesslike of chairmen, suppressing nothing, led the discussion to an innocuous end.

In Brussels such a consummation was relatively easy to achieve. In other countries, where the censorship is intimately concerned with political suppressions, it would not have been so easy, nor did it prove to be so.

Congress followed congress, each separated by a year's national activity, in which Galsworthy played his usual intimate part. After Brussels came Oslo, which Galsworthy was prevented at the last moment from attending; Vienna, where he was received with an overpowering welcome, the more gratifying because he was particularly fond of Austria and chose it for the scene of several of his works—*Villa Rubein*, *The Little Man*, *The Dark Flower*, *The Little Dream*.

Poland came next, and evoked his enthusiasm, for its own sake and because it was the birthplace of Joseph Conrad, one of his very dearest friends. The Arabian Nights hospitality of the Poles was overwhelming. Galsworthy was again chosen as the figure most worthy of special honour, and at the opening ceremony in the Polish parliament building (which was placed at the disposal of the P.E.N. for the period of the congress) it was he who made the formal speech of thanks. I cull a paragraph from a Polish newspaper report of the congress, from which it will be seen that the notion that Galsworthy is the typical Englishman is not confined to this country:

"Some—not all—of these striking heads belong to men whose literary achievements are known not only in their own countries but in the wider sphere of international culture. Foremost is the form of that typical—oh! how typical—English gentleman, John Galsworthy. He is undoubtedly the king of the congress, or, if you will, the sun of the congress-system."

Then followed Holland, where he brought forward the Appeal to Governments on behalf of political and religious prisoners which I have quoted on another page, and, when released from the business and festivities of the occasion, escaped to the picture galleries and feasted his eyes on the Vermeers and other Dutch masterpieces. Jo van Ammers-Küller, the Dutch novelist who is probably best known in England as the author of *The Rebel Generation*, reminds me with what eagerness Galsworthy was besieged by men, women and maidens on his arrival at the first reception. "There was one young girl,"

Photo: W. Zlakowski, Warsaw.

John Galsworthy, Mrs. Dawson Scott and Hermon Ould. Taken in the Parliament House, Warsaw, 1930.

To face p. 92.

she writes, "who asked me to introduce her and she stood before him trembling from emotion and looked at him as she would look to a saint, and I shall never forget his smile of just the tiniest and finest bit of humour and at the same time the extremely kind way he spoke to her." The Galsworthy smile, so gentle, so suddenly illuminating, so inevitably free from malice, is what many will remember him by.

In 1931 the P.E.N. reached its tenth anniversary and Galsworthy, always responsive to incentives which permitted him to sing the praises of friendliness and put another nail in the coffin of war, indulged Mrs. Dawson Scott in her desire to celebrate the occasion. A dinner was held at which twenty-four countries were represented; Galsworthy presided, and once again laid emphasis on his conviction that the P.E.N. should bring writers of all nations in closer and friendlier touch. "There are people who sneer at such aspirations," he said, "but happily I have noticed they are people whose sneers one can positively enjoy. . . . It is thirteen years since the end of the Great War. There is practically no one now alive under the age of eighteen who can remember it except as a tale that is told. And yet its effects and consequences still govern all our lives, occasionally perhaps for the better, almost always for the worse. For five years the nations put their backs into the effort to destroy each other. Can we say that for even one year since, they have put their backs into an effort to recover the ground lost by peace and prosperity? Perhaps the most singular feature of human life is the fact that men, yes and women, in the mass, will show more heroism, self-sacrifice, courage and perseverance in fighting each other than they will show in helping each other . . . My voice carries no

weight, and we are all tired of listening to vague
speeches on this subject. I quite agree we need
action, for with every year that passes, broad resolute
and sustained co-operation among the nations to
understand and lessen each other's economic and
territorial difficulties, to diminish armaments and
treat hostility as a common danger, becomes more
and more imperative."

On this same occasion he again disclaimed the idea
that internationality and nationality were mutually
destructive. "I believe in my own country. I desire
the best for it," he said; "and because of that belief
and that desire I understand how others feel about
their countries. If one is a child in a large family
and wishes to have for oneself all the nubbly bits and
warm corners, or even more than one's fair share of
them, one is commonly called and treated as a pig,
and rightly. I do not know why it should be otherwise in the family of Homo Sapiens, in which the
nations are children. Fair play is a jewel, but I regret
to say that internationally speaking that jewel is
generally at 'My Uncle's,' or, if that expression is too
classical for some of us, let me say—up the spout."

Hungary always held a special charm for him, but
the feelings with which he went to Budapest for the
congress there in 1932 were not undiluted. Europe
was chaotic, and Hungary more chaotic than most
countries. Earlier in the year he had suggested a
postponement of the congress, and, as the political
unrest increased rather than abated, he persisted in
his opinion that it would be better to abandon the
congress rather than risk a fiasco. This point of view
was probably made the more urgent by the fact that
an "invented" interview with him had appeared in a

Hungarian paper, putting into his mouth all sorts of views concerning Hungary and the political situation which he had certainly not expressed and did not even hold. Moreover, his wife's health was causing him some uneasiness, and as he never travelled without her, that added to the uncertainty which hedged the congress about. But more relevant than all, perhaps, the Hungarian P.E.N. itself was apparently suffering from internal combustion which might lead to an explosion at any moment. It was, however, almost an axiom in the P.E.N. never to postpone anything: make a programme and stick to it had become our practice—and nothing was so certain as the uncertainty of European politics. Writing to Hungary I mooted the idea of postponement, but took it for granted that the suggestion would be negatived; and it was so.

The truce between the rival sections of the Hungarian P.E.N. centre was loyally maintained during the week of the congress, the organisers of which worked untold wonders in circumstances which could hardly have been more difficult. Hungarian charm, gypsy orchestras, generous hospitality, pomp and ceremony—all these were there in plenty. Mrs. Galsworthy had recovered in time to make the journey with her husband and enjoyed, with him, the numerous enchantments which imaginative and gracious hosts laid before us. An incident which rests with special vividness in my mind is the reception in the Royal Palace by the Regent, Admiral von Horthy. The magnificence of the building, the superb uniforms of the flunkies, garbed in the manner which we associate with musical comedy, the acres of parquet floors, the ponderous chandeliers burdened with vast quantities of prismatic glass, the cream and silver walls and multiplying mirrors—these remain in the mind like an ornate setting for some eighteenth century fantasy or a Pérrault fairy tale; the note of incongruity is struck by the recollection of groups of dark-suited men and modernly clad women, authors from all over the world, not quite knowing why they were there, waiting to be welcomed by the representative of the Hungarian throne. I stood with the Galsworthys, intensely aware of my own incongruity. Galsworthy, who never liked speech-making, had inevitably been selected to make the speech which introduced the members of the P.E.N. to the Regent, and he stood there, "irreproachably dressed," as they say, somewhat nervous and a little self-conscious. "Don't you leave me, Hermon," he said, as a school-boy might waiting to give an account of himself to an unreasonable task-master. Indeed, there was something especially boyish about him on that occasion: his *savoir faire* was so obviously skin deep, and he was so clearly dubious about the whole proceedings. When the Regent appeared, however, there was nothing in Galsworthy's voice, always clear and well-produced, to betray his nervousness. This is what he said:

"To you in this building of national and historic renown I have the honour to bring a band of pilgrims.

"You, Sir, known to all the world for the staunch fidelity with which you have served your country and your ideals will forgive us for also being people with a star to follow. I will confess to you that our star is hidden. For we of the P.E.N. are not only concerned with promoting from country to country the love and knowledge of literature, but are bound on a

Photo: Schaffer Gy., Budapest.

JOHN GALSWORTHY AND FELIX SALTEN.
P.E.N. Congress in Budapest, May, 1932.

To face p. 96.

long quest for a jewel that has been stolen from the
world, the jewel of friendliness. Wrenched from the
sky where it used to shine—at all events when there
were no momentary thunder-clouds—it is now darkling and fugitive. We pass our days looking for it,
desirous to make it once more a fixed star above a
happier world. Imagine, Sir, how like we are to
Bedouins—wanderers in the desert. Now and again
we are vouchsafed a mirage and see a world of green
pastures and sweet waters, smiling. Now and again
we come to an oasis—such as the oasis of this congress
in Budapest—where the star of friendliness shines on
us as it used to shine everywhere, so far as one could
see. But as a general thing, Sir, and I fear you in
your great experience will admit it—the heavenly
jewel is most thoroughly concealed. Envy, hatred,
and all uncharitableness are a constellation much
more universally conspicuous, not to say admired.

"I have often wondered what is really thought of us
wandering writers of the P.E.N. in the countries we
visit, by all those who are so inexhaustibly polite and
patient with us. Do they secretly think: Who are
these who go about the world with their heads in the
air looking for what is buried in the ground? Believe
me, writers though we be and some of us even cloud-
capped poets—we are capable of appreciating the
courtesy which takes us with the dignified seriousness
usually reserved for ambassadors, financiers and
other stagers of this mortal scene.

"And to you, Sir, and to this your loved country of
Hungary which so long and so bravely served all
Western civilisation by its staunch repulsing of
Eastern encroachment, I feel that we owe it to
explain: That we are not really the dreamers for
which we may be taken, not (I speak for my col-

leagues rather than myself) not 'prigs' and 'humbugs' to use those vigorous and purely English words. No! Underneath this wandering search of ours for the seemingly unattainable, lies a core of commonsense. That which is not searched for is seldom found. Soil which is not tilled will not grow corn. Human life without friendliness is not worth having. And we are perhaps the most practical of mortals, who seek the end that the great masses of mankind desire—a mild and genial air to breathe. We writers of the P.E.N. want to serve humanity at large in the ways (perhaps the only ways) in which the written word and the makers thereof can serve humanity by linking up, country by country, the love of literature, and by helping to restore to a bleak and starved world a friendly atmosphere. And now, Sir, on behalf of us all I thank you, and your gracious country for a greeting and a hospitality that has touched all our hearts."

This is not the place to transcribe the whole of Admiral von Horthy's speech in reply, but a couple of paragraphs may not be superfluous:

"I am familiar with the ideal objects of the Association of the P.E.N. clubs; I know that—apart from endeavouring to unite writers of all nations in one vast family embracing the whole civilised world and thereby to promote the cause of universal culture and to raise the level of our intellectual life—the Association has undertaken to fight for the realisation of the dearest dream of humanity—a world Peace . . .

"It has always been Hungary's ardent wish to become a factor of importance in the promotion of World Peace—of a Peace based on justice and on equal rights for all nations—and to be able to establish close connections with the cultured peoples of Europe whose fates are to-day more closely interwoven than ever before—whose interdependence has never been so manifest as it is under the critical conditions at present prevailing."

To Galsworthy he offered a special welcome. His English was excellent, easy and clearly enunciated. In conversation, after the official ceremonies were over, he said how he would welcome a chance to be back at sea. "Now," he said, "whenever there is a knock at the door, I am afraid to open it because I may be letting in some fresh catastrophe;" and remembering that there are eight hundred and sixty rooms in the Royal Palace, with a corresponding number of knockable doors, the scope for catastrophes seemed almost unlimited.

As I have said, Galsworthy had no love of public speaking, and particularly objected to being asked to speak without notice. He liked to prepare what he had to say beforehand, and frequently committed the greater part of a speech to memory, whether in English, French or German. This must have been due to some sort of eradicable inhibition, for, driven into a corner, he spoke fluently, humorously, and easily. Particularly I remember the post-prandial oration in Budapest when he likened the more prominent members of the P.E.N. there assembled to various animals, who might, in spite of their difference, live together in peace and harmony if they gave their minds to it, deducing therefrom the possibility that the nations of the world, no more intractable than wild beasts and authors, might some day find a way of living without warfare. The speech came from him very effortlessly and spontaneously, accompanied by a ripple of laughter from all who understood it; and it was the last time that Galsworthy addressed an international meeting of the P.E.N.

JOHN GALSWORTHY

There are those who say that a certain pessimism, almost bitterness, had begun to colour Galsworthy's mind at this time, as if he were coming to the conclusion that, after all, the human race was not salvable; and I am not sure that there is not an element of truth in this. He was too old a hand at the game to expect human schemes to follow the course planned for them, and the difficulty of keeping politics out of the P.E.N. would not, in itself, I imagine, seriously disturb him, since the difficulty was one which had been present from the beginning and will remain till the end, needing constant vigilance and disinterested goodwill. An incident which upset him is worth recording, being typical. An appeal had been made to him, as President of the World P.E.N., to make representations to the Hungarian Government on behalf of certain political prisoners who were alleged to be writers and members of the Hungarian P.E.N. Galsworthy, knowing nothing of the merits of the case, never having even heard of the prisoners by name before, refused to involve the P.E.N. in a purely political issue; but after ascertaining as much information as was available, he addressed an eloquent appeal to the Regent, Admiral von Horthy, not as President of the P.E.N. but as John Galsworthy, author. Several newspapers, knowing very little of the circumstances, reported that he had refused to intervene in a matter affecting the lives of certain Hungarian writers, and charged him with various failings among which hypocrisy was not the most offensive. Hardened to misrepresentation as he was, the abuse hurt him no a little.

WE MODERNS

WE MODERNS

"*THE WORLD IS CHANGING, CHANGING* . . ."

THAT there was little depth to the bitterness which Galsworthy occasionally revealed is shown, I think, by his attitude to youth. He liked young people and was charming to them. The "bright young things," in life, in literature and art, amused him and he was apt to say that they made him seem like an old fogey; but there was probably something disingenuous in the confession. Nobody in the fulness of his power as an artist, lacking neither inspiration nor the energy to give it form, really admits that he is old-fashioned. However tentative may have been Galsworthy's salute to the universe in his later work, there is no sign of a flagging creative impulse and in *Flowering Wilderness* and *Over the River* two of his most vital characters, Dinny Charwell and Aunt Em, find their ripest embodiment. He was not, as one says, "set in his ways," except in the sense that he had chosen his method and clung to it, being convinced. He looked upon the work of the more unconventional of his contemporaries with interest—certainly did not condemn it unread—but went his own way. When the P.E.N. entertained Mr. James Joyce in March 1927, Galsworthy gave the function his blessing, but wrote to me at the time: "Joyce really seems to me to be going dotty. I have no patience with this Gollywoggiana stuff." The reference was not to *Ulysses*, of course, but to that *Work in Progress* in which Mr. Joyce fights *à outrance* the battle against conventional expression.

For some of the younger writers Galsworthy had the warmest admiration and many times counselled me to read some novel by a new writer. Mr. H. E. Bates and Mr. Manhood, I remember particularly among his recommendations, and Miss Margaret Kennedy's *The Constant Nymph* earned his blessing within a few days of its appearance. With Mr. Noël Coward's work he was not very familiar, but he was enthusiastic about *Cavalcade* which he thought was a remarkable achievement. Not uncritical of its minor defects, he thought its breadth and grasp remarkable in a young man of Mr. Coward's age and generation. There are several comments on it in *Over the River*. The last words—"Greatness and dignity and peace" —struck the lovelorn Tony as moving and damned ironical, and set him ruminating on the queer incongruities of life; but to Clare, whom he loved, harder than he, more of a realist, it was "sentimental. No country ever had, or will have, greatness and dignity and peace." And later on we find him ruminating: "A country, even one's own, was a mish-mash of beauties and monstrosities, a vague generalisation that betrayed dramatists into over-writing, journalists into blurb." Clare's comment on the honeymoon couple leaning over the rail of the Titanic, unmindful of their doom, is not without point: "It didn't look to me as if their love would have lasted long. They were eating each other like sugar."

I shall be forgiven, I hope, if I quote the first letter I ever received from Galsworthy; it shows the open-mindedness towards modern methods of one who was himself content to follow a more traditional course. The play referred to is *The Dance of Life*, then running

at the King's Theatre, Hammersmith. The letter is
dated July 4th, 1925.

"By and large I was delighted with your play,
especially with the Brendle scene, the cell, and the
hill-top. That was in itself a justification of your
method. I suppose the first interlude (dream) may
be said to help a little; and the bit of dream on the
knife-board a little, but it is not till we get to the
hill-top that the real value and possibility break on
one and convince. I draw from the interludes this
moral: that this method of yours demands, of the
interlude, fancy and inspiration to give it—the
interlude—a life of its own and make it not merely
a talking-on of the scene before. You want as it
were the shadows to play a little at an angle to
the action of their waking selves. I like the play in
other ways, too. I like its philosophy. Altogether
I came away happy, and so did my wife."

This is at least evidence that Galsworthy was not
antagonistic to innovations as such, but only to
innovations which seemed to be introduced for the
sake of novelty and not because they were the
inevitable vehicle for the artist's purpose. For the
clever-clever type of young man or woman who
began to sprout during the war and to blossom soon
after the armistice, he had no great liking; cliques
which existed mainly to glorify their component
parts and criticise rival cliques, excited his scornful
amusement, and art and conduct which, despising
roots, came into being by a process of spontaneous
generation seemed to him likely to peter out with
similar effortlessness. "Take my tip, Fleur," says
Michael Mont in *The White Monkey*; "the really big

people don't talk and don't bunch—they paddle their own canoes in what seem backwaters. But it's the backwaters that make the main stream."

His estimate of the post-war generation is crystallised in *The White Monkey*. The Chinese picture which gave the book its name showed a large whitish monkey, whiskered, with almost human eyes, holding the rind of a squeezed fruit in one of its paws. "Eat the fruits of life, scatter the rinds, and get copped doing it," it seemed to say. "The human tragedy incarnate . . . He thinks there's something beyond, and he's sad or angry because he can't get at it." Disillusionment, cynicism, hopelessness—these seemed to Galsworthy to be characteristic of the generation most articulate during the first decade after the war. Fleur, true daughter of Soames and Annette, was also the daughter of the Age and her point of view was one to which innumerable of her contemporaries would have subscribed: "Life! . . . we don't believe anything can last. . . . Of course, there's art, but most of us aren't artists; besides, expressionism—Michael says it's got no inside." This cynicism without bitterness is shown by Fleur's willingness to deceive her husband, have an affair with Jon behind Michael's back, concealing the intrigue for his own sake, she would say, thus disavowing any abstract principles of conduct; and by her assumption, too, that if the little model, Victorine, had allowed herself to be seduced by the painter, she would not betray the fact to her husband. Similarly, Amabel Nazing did not mind her husband flying to Paris with Marjorie Ferrar, but she did object to not having been told beforehand, so that she herself might have flown to Paris with somebody else. Marjorie Ferrar herself, rather deeper in cynicism than most of them, had some sort of code, which she discovered in a moment of self-revelation: "Not to let a friend down; not to give a man away; not to funk; to do things differently from other people; to be always on the go; not to be stuffy; not to be dull."

Michael Mont, idealist, without moral flaw, a "sympathetic" character, with a lively social conscience, expresses a concern which no doubt echoes Galsworthy's own, and being a publisher he has some opportunity for seeing what people are writing if not what they are thinking. He reads some poems, finds them bitter as quinine. The unrest in them—the yearning behind the words! "What is it?" he asks himself. "What's wrong with us? We're quick, and clever, cocksure, and dissatisfied . . . We've chucked religion, tradition, property, pity; and in their place we put—what? Beauty? Gosh!" He goes with Fleur to a nightclub, and beholds vacuity! But "this is a vacuous age—didn't you know?" asks Fleur. "Is there no limit?"—"A limit is what you can't go beyond;" says Fleur; "one can always become more vacuous." They watch a couple dancing, wobbling towards them with their knees flexed as if their souls had slipped down into them; their eyes regarded Fleur and Michael with no more expression than could have been found in four first-class marbles. A strange earnestness radiated from them below the waist, but above that line they seemed to have passed away. "I refuse to believe," says Michael, "that this represents our Age—no beauty, no joy, no skill, not even devil! Just look a fool and wobble your knees!"

The general strike of 1926 seemed to provide grounds for an abatement of cynicism: a great national crisis can be relied upon to unite masses or classes in common fear or common assertiveness. *Swan Song* opens at this period and Galsworthy recreates the curious atmosphere which prevailed when an easily-earned heroism was available for those who, ordinarily clean, might attain glory through dirt. A gentleman who, for love and out of a sense of duty, stoked an engine which had been deserted by a striker who habitually stoked it for a living, was lauded for his patriotism; and young Jon, having missed the Great War, felt that he could not afford to miss this. I am not sure that the sentimentality and self-righteousness which characterised this period were preferable to the easy cynicism which preceded it and returned as soon as the strike was over.

But perhaps we may take heart of grace from one thing—the apparent permanence of the maternal instinct. Even Fleur's cynicism and detachment drop from her, at any rate temporarily, when the advent of the "eleventh baronet" is imminent. It is an amusing touch, and sound psychologically, which makes her decide to change the colour of her bedroom curtains to blue. "They say blue has an effect on the mind—the present curtains really are too jazzy."

BROADCASTING

Towards the material developments due to modern science Galsworthy maintained a certain aloofness. In November 1932, when he and Mrs. Dawson Scott and I had to attend an international committee of the P.E.N. in Paris, I told him that we, being pressed for time, had decided to fly over: would he fly too? The firmness with which he replied in the negative left no doubt about his aversion even from

"WINGSTONE," GALSWORTHY'S HOME IN DEVONSHIRE.

Left to right: H. Granville-Barker, Lillah McCarthy, G. Bernard Shaw, Mrs. Shaw, Mrs. Galsworthy, John Galsworthy. Probably 1912 or 1913.

To face p. 108.

the thought of this form of locomotion. And it will be remarked that any references to aeroplanes and airships in his work have relation to their baneful function in time of war, instruments of destruction, spreaders of bombs and poison gas.

He was sceptical, too, about the gramophone and the wireless. My encomiums on the former influence him a little, and he said that if I could, hand on heart, recommend an instrument which would not outrage the sensibility of a music-lover, he was willing to put aside his prejudices and instal one at Bury House. I made my recommendation, but the projected visit to the makers, like so many other schemes, failed to materialise owing to lack of time. As a matter of fact, there was a gramophone in an obscure corner of Bury House, a somewhat commonplace table-model, and on one occasion we listened to a record of the "Two Black Crows," over which Galsworthy chuckled a great deal.

Radio music also left him cold; and it was some time before he would consent to the broadcasting of one of his plays. It was I who broke down this prejudice. An official of the British Broadcasting Corporation asked me if I would approach Galsworthy about broadcasting *Strife*; all advances hitherto had failed. My own experiences of radio drama were of the scantiest. A few of my own shorter plays had been broadcast but I had not listened-in to them, and I clung to the conviction that only plays which had been designed for broadcasting should be used. The adaptation of one form to the medium of another always seemed to me inexpedient, and the few examples of radio drama which I knew had not impressed me. I was therefore not the best possible advocate! But, thought I, if plays written for the theatre are going to be broadcast, it would be as well to broadcast the best plays, and not only was *Strife* a good play, but its sane demonstration of the futility of industrial strife seemed peculiarly designed to instruct a country in the toils of industrial unrest.

Galsworthy was abroad when the request came to me from the B.B.C., but I was meeting him in Warsaw, and it was over lunch at the Jugoslav Legation, when I was sitting next to Galsworthy, that I found the first chance of broaching the subject. I remember that his first impulse was to refuse his permission out of hand; his second to refer the matter to his agents (to whom, I suspect, he had given general instructions of a negative character); but when I emphasised the social value of broadcasting *Strife*—which, by the way, he considered his best play—his resistance broke down and he gave his consent. Ironically enough, although it was I who was directly responsible for the first broadcast of *Strife*, I have never listened-in to a Galsworthy play. Some months later he was asked—again through me, but this time I saw no reason for supporting the claim—to write a play especially for broadcasting, and he refused.

MUSIC

It is easy enough to understand his disinclination to listen-in to music. To inveterate concert-goers, no little part of the enjoyment comes from the setting in which the music is given. The crowded hall, the buzz of excitement, peculiarly infectious among music enthusiasts; the tuning of the instruments; the projection of the personality of conductor, singer, player; the great drama of the concerto, when the protagonist soloist takes the centre of the stage—leaps, as it were, into the arena, and the conductor and orchestra are held at bay for an intense half-an-hour —all this is lost in the privacy of listening-in, however accurate the loud speaker, however restrained the atmospherics.

"By the cigars they smoke and the composers they love, ye shall know the texture of men's souls." Thus, without preamble, Galsworthy lays down the law in that most perfect of his shorter works, *Indian Summer of a Forsyte*. Having no more than an academic interest in smoking I failed to notice the labels on the cigars which Galsworthy smoked; but closed eyes bring up a vision of him puffing at a weed (if that belittling word is not out of place) that appeared to give him that air of serenity and satisfaction which more than her accustomed quantity of milk gives a cat. By deduction I know that he smoked mild cigars, be-cause old Jolyon could not bear a strong cigar or Wagner's music, and as Galsworthy shared his dis-like of the latter, it may be assumed that he shared his preference for the former.

Galsworthy's interest in music was constant and his taste definite; but his attitude was not the atti-tude of the professional musician, and he had very little technical knowledge. Musical metaphors are not infrequently employed by him, sometimes rather pointlessly, but often aptly. His work is almost completely free from musical howlers. I only recall a couple. Gyp (*Beyond*), who being some-thing of a musician ought to have known better, "did not realise how she had grown up in these few days, how the ground bass had already come into the light music of her life;" and Miltoun (*The Patrician*) meditating on London, thinks of it as a great discordant symphony of sharps and flats, which shows he was no musician. One is inevitably reminded of Tennyson's busy little brook which chattered over stony ways "in little sharps and trebles," presumably in order to find a rhyme for pebbles. But two ineptitudes are a modest gleaning from thirty volumes scattered about which are numerous allusions to music. Musicians pop in and out of his pages, and one of his chief characters, Fiorsen in *Beyond*, is a professional violinist. Not a very estimable individual, consumed with self-pity and completely unstable— one hopes that Fiorsen did not stand in Galsworthy's mind as typical of the musical executant.

It is always interesting to observe how music affects the non-professional listener, for in no art is the cleavage between professional and non-professional so wide. It is almost as if their organs of hearing were differently constructed. To the professional musician music is not "like" anything else: it is itself. The non-professional is always at pains to liken it to something not itself. Gyp is stirred uncannily by the playing of Fiorsen. He had remarkable technique, we are informed, and the intense wayward feeling of his playing was chiselled by it, as if a flame were being frozen in its swaying—an image, surely, which nobody whose job was music would employ, but expressive enough.

Some of Galsworthy's preferences are certainly identical with those of old Jolyon, who loved Beethoven, Mozart, Handel, Gluck and Schumann, but I have no reason to believe that he, like old Jolyon, Joseph Conrad and his own father, had any enthusiasm for the operas of Meyerbeer. In the matter of operas one was indisputably his favourite, Bizet's *Carmen*. Long ago he spoke to me excitedly about it.

"Such a jolly good story," he said with almost boyish enthusiasm, "and such perfect tunes!" It was some time later that Mrs. Galsworthy and he decided to make an English translation of the libretto which should be more practicable, from the singer's point of view, than that quaint version which, with almost comical perversity, puts all the accents in the wrong places. The fruit of this labour of love was published only a few months before his death. Miss Ursula Greville, who went over the whole thing with him to make sure that every line was singable, told me how indefatigably he applied himself to the task, allowing neither her nor himself any rest until the whole text had been thoroughly overhauled.

It will be remembered that *Carmen* was Wilfrid Desert's favourite opera and had a special significance for Dinny his ill-starred beloved. "The Habanera! What a shiver its first notes always gave one! How wild, sudden, strange and inescapable was love! *L'amour est enfant de Bohême!*" And she goes on brooding on life and love and loneliness, until she is roused again by the Toreador's song. "A blot on the opera, it's most popular tune!" she thinks; and then corrects her first thought, remembering that it was meant to blare above the desolation of that tragic end, as the world blared around the passion of lovers. The world was a heedless and heartless stage for lives to strut across, or in dark corners join and cling together. . . . Perhaps she remembered, too, that Bizet expressed his own purpose very clearly by demanding that the Toreador's song should be sung *avec grand fatuité*.

For opera in general Galsworthy cared little. It is, he thought, a mongrel form, and one had always to be making allowances for it, giving it only a half-

willing credence instead of the complete surrender
which a work of art has the right to demand. Against
Carmen, however, he would hear no criticism.
"*Carmen* was a vice with us both," he once said,
coupling himself with Conrad. For *Pagliacci*, too, he
had a special affection—again, probably, because
the story took possession of the music and fused with
it perfectly; the music of Gluck's *Orfeo* always
evoked his enthusiasm and "Che Faro?" was to him
one of the greatest melodies ever written. It was
"Che Faro?" that Fiorsen played when he seized
the fiddle out of a beggar's hands one evening off
Piccadilly. "I'll make some money for you," he said.
"He played wonderfully on that poor fiddle; and the
fiddler, who had followed at his elbow, stood watching, uneasy, envious, a little entranced. This tall,
pale, monsieur with the strange face and the
drunken eyes and hollow chest, played like an
angel!" But even a genius performing in a Piccadilly
bystreet may miscalculate his drawing-power. Fiorsen was met with drawn curtains and closing windows like any derelict scraper-out of unwanted tunes.
It was "Che Faro?" too, that Irene played for old
Jolyon when Chopin's charms had been momentarily exhausted.

If you mentioned Wagner, Galsworthy shook his
head, murmured his agreement with the later
Nietzsche, and let it go at that. In *The Island Pharisees* something of his real feelings on the subject are
shown. Two American ladies, assembled under the
tent of hair belonging to a writer of songs, were dis-
cussing the emotions aroused in them by Wagner's
operas.

"They projuice a strange condition of affairs in
me," said the thinner one.

"They're just divine," said the fatter.

"I don't know if you can call the fleshly lusts divine," replied the thinner, looking into the eyes of the writer of songs.

I suppose it was Bach whom he placed on the supreme altitude. "He's a grand chap," he said; and once, when a young musician friend of mine, David Carver, declared his preference for Beethoven, Galsworthy replied: "I used to think like that, but wait till you're ten years older: you'll come to Bach" —for which assumption of superiority he was promptly chidden by his wife. Notwithstanding this preference for Bach, his books contain very few allusions to him. One reference has a peculiar interest, owing to its side-light on war-time mentality. A concert is in progress at Queen's Hall; the second number, which, in spite of all the efforts of patriotism, was of German origin—a Brandenburg concerto by Bach. More curious still, it was encored. Certainly the repetition of a Brandenburg concerto, even the Third, would be something of a novelty, in peace-time or war-time. Was Galsworthy calling on his imagination, I wonder, or did Sir Henry Wood share in the prevailing habit of giving the Tommies whatever they wanted, cigarettes or concertos?

Before he had placed Bach on the loftiest pedestal, I imagine it was Beethoven who occupied that position, and the Seventh Symphony came highest in his esteem. Courtier (*The Patrician*) described it as the finest piece of music ever written and dragged the haughty patrician Miltoun, conscience-ridden and somewhat bitter, into Queen's Hall to listen to it. The great lighted hall, filled with the faint blueish vapour from hundreds of little rolls of tobacco leaf, was crowded from floor to ceiling. . . . The first slow

notes of the Seventh Symphony of Beethoven had
begun to steal forth across the bank of flowers; and
save for the steady rising of that blueish vapour, as
it were incense burnt to the god of melody, the
crowd had become deadly still, as though one mind,
one spirit, possessed each pale face inclined towards
that music rising and falling like the sighing of the
winds, that welcome from death the freed spirits of
the beautiful. "Hasn't that shown you how things
swell and grow; how splendid the world is?" asks
Courtier, and Miltoun answers: "It has shown me
how beautiful the world can be made by a great
man."

It was the slow movement from Beethoven's
Seventh that so profoundly moved the Reverend
Edward Pierson, that unhappy believer doomed to
function in an age of unbelief. To him, I fear, music
was in many ways a narcotic, an escape from reality,
a substitute for living. Whenever circumstances
overwhelmed him it was to music that he turned
for solace, as the coarser-fibred turn to drink. Tin-
tern Abbey to him was lovely like a great piece of
music, for he put everything into music; and when
his love for his daughter seems to overwhelm him,
he goes to the piano and plays Mendelssohn's Prelude
and Fugue in E minor with a sort of dreamy passion.
It was his way out of perplexities, regrets and longings; a way which never quite failed him. He finds
the modern sceptical spirit insupportable; turns to
his little old piano, touches the shabby keys, and
sings in a worn voice: "Holy, holy, holy, Merciful
and Mighty." He finds himself bewildered by the
sudden change of relationship between him and his
daughter . . . slips away; mounts to the organ loft
of his church, plays softly modulating chords "wan-

dering into each other." And on that occasion when the Bach concerto was encored at Queen's Hall, his favourite piece of music, the César Franck violin sonata, is performed. What insight Galsworthy showed in linking up César Franck with this sympathetic but rather futile clergyman, left over, as it were, from a previous generation; Franck, with his never-ending yearning and somewhat too-consciously worked-up exultation! The sonata brought Pierson a view of heaven, of devotional blue air where devout stars were shining in a sunlit noon, above ecstatic trees and waters where ecstatic swans were swimming. . . . When, under the bludgeoning of fate, he gives up his church, it is to music that he flies for comfort. Of all that he would leave, he would miss this most— the right to come and play here in the darkening church, to release emotional sound in this dim empty space growing ever more beautiful. From chord to chord he let himself go deeper and deeper into the surge and swell of those sound waves, losing all sense of actuality, till the music and the whole dark building were fused in one rapturous solemnity.

Chopin—the counterpart in music of the remote and lovely Irene—is often evoked by Galsworthy. It was one of Chopin's nocturnes which had so unhappy an effect upon the dog celebrated in *Memories*: he always whimpered when he heard it. Music in general made him restless, inclined to sigh, and to ask questions. Sometimes, at its first sound, he would cross to the window and remain there looking for his mistress. At others, he would simply go and lie on the loud pedal, and they never could tell whether it was from sentiment, or because he thought that in this way he heard less.

Except for one passing allusion in *Over the River*, I

do not remember any reference to Brahms. This is strange, for Galsworthy was a great Brahmsian, holding back only from the Fourth Symphony. The songs delighted him and "Muss es Eine Trennung geben" from the Magelone Lieder seemed to him one of the most beautiful songs ever written; his nephew, Rudolf Sauter, would play it on the flute for his delight. I always remember with amazement an evening at Bury when, quite unprecedentedly, I burst into song. At dinner I had rather crudely mimicked a typical bass singing Handel's "O ruddier than the cherry", upon which Galsworthy surprisingly decided that I must be made to sing when we got to the drawing-room. I withdrew behind the absence of music, but a few volumes of Lieder were produced and I sang some of the Schumann "Dichterliebe" to my own inadequate accompaniment. Then Mrs. Galsworthy—a trained musician and excellent sight-reader—offered to play for me, with the usual result when enthusiastic amateurs are let loose: we went on playing and singing for hours—Schumann, Brahms, and, I think, Schubert —unmindful of the time and even, I fear, of Galsworthy, who, at midnight, quietly decreed that it was bed-time.

CRAFTSMAN

REFORMER IN PLAY AND NOVEL; IN-NOVATOR; TYPES AND INDIVIDUALS

THE reformer in Galsworthy is as evident in the plays as in the novels, but in little else do these two sides of his genius meet. There are a few passages in the novels which might, without alteration, be incorporated in some unwritten play—little scenes whose effectiveness on the stage can be visualised, pages of dialogue, particularly in the later novels, which only a dramatist could have written. From such indications his capacity for writing a play might have been deduced if he had never written one. But his novels could not be justly described, as Bernard Shaw's might have been, as a playwright's novels, nor his plays, as George Moore's might have been, as a novelist's plays. In both forms he wrote as to the manner born; the integrity of each art is perfectly preserved. Chronologically, he was first a novelist, his first considerable novel, *The Island Pharisees*, appearing in 1904, and his first play, *The Silver Box*, not until 1906, when it was one of the most significant features of the famous Vedrenne-Barker season at the Court Theatre.

Galsworthy the reformer was present in both of these works; the social conscience of their author has never been more clearly revealed. But whereas *The Island Pharisees* is, technically, a somewhat poor piece of work, tentative, groping, the characters for the most part only half realised, *The Silver Box* shows the surest of hands from the moment when the curtain rises on a carefully prepared scene till it falls on one of the most moving of climaxes. There is only one doubtful episode in the play; when the little son of the charwoman, Mrs. Jones—temporarily orphaned because his mother has been taken into custody on a false charge—sobs outside the house of the Barthwicks. Our nerves are already on edge, and this final turn of the screw might perhaps be regarded as hitting below the belt. The play—unique in its generation for its quiet naturalism and restraint—does not need this extra stress.

Galsworthy himself seems to have been a little uneasy about the scene, and Mr. Ford Madox Ford has recorded a meeting with him after the second performance. "He sketched several endings and rejected them," says Mr. Ford. "The point was that a middle-class woman, amiable but insensitive, had had the mother of the child arrested on the wrongful suspicion of having stolen the silver cigarette box. The child, finding that its mother did not come home, hung to the railings outside the open window and cried for her, and the scene ended on the sound of the wailing." Mr. Ford made the somewhat frivolous suggestion that the middle-class woman might send the child out a slice of cake, and for the first time in his life found Galsworthy become really heated. "He came out of the depths of his abstraction to say that that was an atrocious suggestion. The woman was a decent, well brought-up mother. Her maternal instincts—the maternal instincts of any woman—would let her know that a slice of cake was not a fitting substitute for a mother's care." Mr. Ford's curious comment on this little reminiscence is: "So perhaps his detachment from the class that he so constantly held up to scorn was not so absolute as it might seem." It is puzzling that anybody who knew Galsworthy as well as Mr. Ford did, should have entertained the idea that he was "detached" from the middle-class to which he belonged. Surely his attacks on the shibboleths and fetishes of the middle-class derive the greater part of their force from the closeness of his contact with it.

The Silver Box brought something new to the English theatre—indeed to the theatre of the world. Naturalism—or realism as it was more commonly called in those days—had already begun to find adherents. Gerhardt Hauptmann in Germany, Antoine's Théâtre Libre in France, Ibsen, Bjornson and Strindberg in Scandinavia, had cut adrift from the artificiality of the latter part of the nineteenth century, and Miss Horniman in Manchester, following her peculiar bent, had encouraged a school of realistic playwrights who enriched our dramatic literature. But Galsworthy, in *The Silver Box*, was different from all of these. So-called photographic realism was never his aim, and genre pictures in the manner of the Manchester school would never have inspired him to emulation. With the earliest plays of Hauptmann—*Die Weber*, for instance—he had more affinity, but Hauptmann painted with wider strokes, was less concerned with verisimilitude and more with the expression of a fundamentally poetic temperament. With the perfervid work of Strindberg Galsworthy had little in common, and even Ibsen, with his predilection for strange remote characters and situations, his symbolism, and ultimate mysticism, touched Galsworthy only at comparatively unimportant points. *The Silver Box* broke new ground in several ways. Although apparently naturalistic, its dialogue is very conscious and selective; consecrated to the revelation of the theme of the play, it never deviates from this purpose in order to throw sidelights on a class or breaks into irrelevancies in order to amuse or to impress by fine words. Galsworthy calls the play, somewhat ironically, "a comedy," and there is indeed a good deal that is amusing in it, but such humour as it possesses is not introduced for its own sake but belongs to the characterisation; it is for the most part concentrated in the fatuous self-complacency of Mrs. Barthwick and her self-righteous husband whose inability to see themselves as others see them leads them to express themselves with unconscious humour. Mrs. Barthwick is convinced that socialists are an absolutely selfish set of people, and the expression of her conviction, amusing in its very humourlessness, is therefore true to character:

"I've no patience with your talk of reform—all that nonsense about social policy . . . Those socialists . . . they have no sense of patriotism like the upper classes; *they simply want what we've got.*"

And:

"MRS. BARTHWICK. You don't look things in the face."

"MR. BARTHWICK. Indeed! I am a Liberal. Drop the subject, please!"

And once again to her husband: "Your principles are nothing in the world but sheer fright," and to her guilty son: "We want you to speak the truth and say you never let this low man into the house."

An innovation, too, was the quietness of the "curtains." The three scenes of the first act—a construction, by the way, which must have seemed revolutionary to the believers in the well-made play of tradition, with its three or four undivided acts—

IRENE ROOKE
as Mrs. Jones in *The Silver Box*.

MILTON ROSMER
as Jones in *The Silver Box*.

To face p. 124

end so unobtrusively that when the curtain falls on them one has the sort of sensation that one might have if one had been peering through a window and the occupant of the room had quietly drawn the blind. There is no climax, and yet the necessary tension is maintained. And the final curtain must be one of the least contrived in all dramatic literature.

"MAGISTRATE. We will now adjourn for lunch!
MRS. JONES (turning to him with a humble gesture). Oh! Sir!——

Barthwick hesitates, then yielding to his nerves, he makes a shamefaced gesture of refusal, and hurries out of Court. Mrs. Jones stands looking after him."

This is not the end of Mrs. Jones, but it is the end of the play. The curtain falls, but life goes on. The very point of the play is indeed in this: that Mrs. Jones, guiltless, is left to bear the brunt of circumstances which she could in no way control, the victim of a law which nominally leaves her unpunished; and if we do not, after the final curtain, follow her in our imagination and face with her the problem of life, the play has failed. It is the author's triumph that we do follow her.

But perhaps the thing which chiefly distinguished the play, and proclaimed that a new personality had entered the English theatre, was the introduction into the dramatis personæ of an impersonal force— the Law, as much a character as Mrs. Jones herself. The parts which the Gods played in the works of the great Greek dramatists, are played in Galsworthy's plays by abstract forces and institutions. The Law dominates more than one of his plays; the Mob dominates others; the Sense of Property, others. It is the same with the novels. The Land is the heroine of

The Freelands; the crumbling structure of the governing classes plays a leading role in *The Patrician*; the predatory instincts of the middle classes are the warp and woof of the Forsyte chronicles, and so on.

Whether the first creative impulse in Galsworthy's mind when he started to write *The Silver Box* came from the conception of the charwoman heroine, Mrs. Jones, or from the pained contemplation of the operations of the Law as it affected the rich and the poor, is relatively unimportant: it is undoubtedly the Law which plays the leading role. An author is rarely able to trace the seed which germinated into a work of art; he is himself as inescapably in the hands of outside forces as his characters are in his. Galsworthy is said to have denied that *Strife* arose from meditating on the facts of the industrial system which permits men of fine calibre to waste themselves in a war of attrition in which both lose. "The play arose in Mr. Galsworthy's mind from his actually having seen in conflict the two men who were the prototypes of Anthony and Roberts, and thus noted the waste and inefficacy arising from the clash of strong characters unaccompanied by balance. It was accident that led him to place the two men in an environment of capital and labour. In reality, both of them were, if not capitalists, at any rate on the side of capital." Thus William Archer. Be this as it may, once having begun on *Strife* any preconceptions born of theory went to the winds, and, although the human interest of the play is fastened on to Anthony and Roberts, the protagonist is really the modern industrial system.

It is only necessary to glance at a list of Galsworthy's plays to see how consistently he adhered to this practice, whatever may have been the immediate springs of action. The characters in *The Eldest Son* are interesting for their own sakes, and had they existed in another plot they would still have made their appeal; but in this play the god who rules their destinies is the god of Caste, and again it is the social conventions which play the determining part. *Justice* is not only the title but the chief character in the only one of his plays which Galsworthy called a tragedy. "Justice" is, indeed, the god of Greek tragedy, who makes of man a plaything and finally crushes him. *The Mob* again bears the protagonist's name in the title. *The Forest* symbolises the imperialistic jungle in which men lose their individuality, overwhelmed by its blind power. And similarly with most of the other plays.

The practice has obvious dangers. Characters over whom impersonal forces hover hawk-like waiting to pounce, may lose their freedom of will; and freedom of will is, to a character in a play or a novel, the breath of life. Characters must run their course according to their inherent qualities, and not according to some prearranged scheme of a playwright who wishes to prove a thesis. Some of Galsworthy's characters, it must be confessed, are inhibited by the rigidity of their author's construction: there is not enough *give* in them—they are truer to themselves than anybody ever is! But there are relatively few characters in this category. In general, in spite of the water-tight construction, the characters move freely and vividly. The playwright Galsworthy must have had to resist many temptations to create subtle and complex characters, applying to the drama a gift which he felt should be reserved for the novel. Characters in a play, he thought, ought to be clearly and suggestively defined, but the theatrical medium did not admit of the finer shades of characterisation:

127

the personality of the actor was always an unknown quantity upon which the playwright's conception must be superimposed, and subtlety would therefore be wasted. There is much truth in this generalisation, and although I think Galsworthy carried it too far, truncating his imagination in deference to a theory, I am bound to confess that within the limits which he imposed upon himself, he managed to create a vast number of characters, many of whom only just miss that uniqueness which is the glory of the Soames, the Aunt Ems, the Margery Pendyces, the Dinny Charwells, the Fleurs, Jolyons, Mr. Stones, and Mirandas of the novels.

His gift of giving the essentials of a character in a few words, putting an intelligent actor in possession of just those details which it is his duty to convey, must be unsurpassed. Strangway, in *A Bit o' Love*, is "a gentle creature, burnt within." "A faint smile hovers about his lips that Nature has made rather full and he has made thin." Hornblower (*Skin Game*) is "thoroughly broadened, blown out, as it were by success." "He carries a Homburg hat, which one suspects will look too small on his head." Clare (*The Fugitive*) has "full, smiling lips, and large grey mesmeric eyes; one of those women all vibration iced over with a trained stoicism of voice and manner." Minor characters are particularly neatly sketched, as if the author were anxious lest their relative unimportance should lead to careless characterisations. "James Home (*The Mob*), a thin, tall, grey-bearded man, with plentiful hair, contradictory eyebrows, and the half-shy, half-bold manners, alternately rude and over-polite, of one not accustomed to Society, yet secretly much taken with himself." "Charles Shelder (*The Mob*) with a bald egg-shaped head, and gold pince-nez. He has little side whiskers, a leathery, yellowish skin, a rather kind but watchful and dubious face, and when he speaks seems to have a plum in his mouth, which arises from the preponderance of his shaven upper lip." And there are dozens of similar swift outline drawings scattered about the plays, revealing not only Galsworthy's acute gift of observation and power to reconstruct what he observed, but what is more to the present point, his exact knowledge of how to exploit the actor's art to his own end.

The economy of his method, never brimming over; the restraint of his dialogue, with its "H'ms", "Oh, sirs!" and "Well, I'm . . . s"; the absence of long speeches—except in the Court scenes—might have been expected to allow for unusual fluidity and expansion: the contrary is the case. A hundred intelligent actors might reveal a hundred legitimate Hamlets, for all the copiousness of Shakespeare's dialogue; Mr. Shaw's St. Joan, notwithstanding her historical roots, appeals differently to every actress who essays the part—there is the saintly country wench of Dame Sybil Thorndike, the pathetic child of Madame Pitoieff, the inspired but bewildered girl of Elisabeth Bergner, the swashbuckleress of the modern Russian theatre. But the possible variations on the Galsworthy big roles are few. Norman McKinnel's Anthony in *Strife* was the essential Anthony, from which no other actor's interpretation would greatly differ; the Mrs. Jones of Irene Rooke, of Ada King, of Nancy Price have shades of difference accounted for by the different personalities of the actresses, but their *interpretation* of all three is practically identical, varied by an extra touch of pathos there, an added emphasis there, but not by any real difference of conception. And so, in a greater or a less degree, with all Galsworthy's characters. The mould is not to be tampered with, but, the cast once made, polishing and finishing touches are left to the artist.

Virtuosity in a Galsworthy role is therefore almost out of the question. Given sound acting, the plays are sure of their effect. In almost all of those which preceded and include *Escape*, the author's instinct for the theatre, his water-tight construction, the intrinsic interest of his material, and his passionate sense of message, may be relied upon to carry an audience; and undue emphasis or extravagance in acting would inevitably destroy the balance of Galsworthy's conception and blemish the semblance of naturalism which is his outstanding contribution to dramatic art, as colours added by brush to a wood-engraving would destroy its essential character. One remembers how the flamboyant art of Mr. Ernest Milton was confined within the bounds of Galsworthy's conception of Ferdinand de Levis (*Loyalties*) and what power it derived from the constraint; if it had slipped its bonds and indulged its natural tendency to extravagance, De Levis would have ceased to be De Levis and the equilibrium of *Loyalties* would have been displaced. It is sometimes said that the plays of Mr. Shaw are fool-proof, because, granting good enunciation on the part of the actor, the text will do the rest. Almost the reverse is true of Galsworthy's characters. Galsworthy claims the co-operation of the actor; he demands good characterisation from the beginning, and the text is in many cases the least important ingredient in the creation of desired effect. There are not many Galsworthy roles in which an actor may hope to score a spectacular success; but

MEGGIE ALBANESI
A photograph taken just before she died

To face p. 130.

there are innumerable roles which provide excellent material for good, effective acting and the satisfaction of having assisted at the creation of a real human being. Some of our soundest actors are almost inevitably associated in one's mind with the plays of Galsworthy—the lamented Norman McKinnel, the no less lamented Meggie Albanesi, Irene Rooke, Milton Rosmer, Ada King, J. Fisher White, J. H. Roberts, Edmund Gwenn, Leon M. Lion, Lawrence Hanray.

No later play of Galsworthy is so quiet and delicate in its technique as *The Silver Box*; with *The Skin Game* he seems to have decided to use a somewhat coarser method. True the subject demanded broader strokes and louder stresses, but as subsequent plays— *The Show*, for example—might have been treated in *The Silver Box* manner and were not, it may be assumed that he decided that the post-war age demanded more forceful methods. It must not be forgotten that in the theatre Galsworthy was first and last a reformer: there is hardly a play of his which was not intended to convey a message—a lesson, if you will. The reformer in him would therefore have deemed it sheer stupidity to write plays in a medium so subtle that their purport eluded the minds of the general public, when it was the general public whose conscience he wished to rouse. He reserved for his novels his sensitive appreciation of the finer shades of human character and the infinite variety of human experience. To his plays he brought talents more commonly associated with craft than with art. He had the ability to construct a play flawlessly, so that all its parts are related to the whole, and the whole is perfectly poised. In some cases the scheme might almost be given diagrammatically. This in itself is not an unusual gift; the authors of many a machine-made play could boast as much. Where they fail, however, is in making the audience more aware of the machinery than of the play, whereas in Galsworthy's work the machinery is no more than a skeleton well out of sight. The parallelism of *The Silver Box*, for instance, to which I have referred : how exact it is, and yet how naturally it works ! The desire of the author was to show that the Law, although nominally unbiassed, bears more hardly on the poor than on the rich. He interweaves the fortunes of the two families : the middle-class Barthwicks and the lower-class Joneses. Mrs. Jones is charwoman to Mrs. Barthwick. The son of Mrs. Barthwick, being drunk, takes the reticule of a street-girl—for fun, to score off her. The husband of Mrs. Jones, being drunk, takes a silver cigarette box from the sitting-room of the Barthwicks, out of spite. There is no reason why either of these incidents should not have taken place; as they are presented they convince and we ask no questions. The juxtaposition of these two purloinings was exactly what Galsworthy needed to enable him to develop his theme; it was important that the two cases should be almost exactly similar, neither the rich man nor the poor man guilty of any but a technical offence; it was important that the lives of the two sets of characters should be interwoven, so that the structure of the play might be more compact and the moral the more poignant. To have linked these episodes, exploited these coincidences, without provoking awkward questions in the mind of the onlooker shows an unusual mastery of a difficult method; to do this and have your play classified in subsequent histories of the drama as a classic specimen of the naturalistic method, a supreme example of what is very unfairly called the photographic school of realism, is a triumph indeed.

The Silver Box does not stand alone in this respect. Indeed most of the plays are similarly closely woven, though not all of them so deftly. *Loyalties* is a model of its kind. The statement of the situation in the first scene could hardly have been more concise or more provocative; the atmosphere becomes taut at once, and the tension is maintained, with little letting-up, until the end of the play. Once more we have a case of an abstract idea dominating the whole work: the idea of loyalty—to class, to club, to friends, to employer, to wife, to husband, to one's profession, to the traditions of the army. Galsworthy was amazingly fecund in inventing situations which enabled him to rub in his moral; but even more amazing was his skill in combining them all in one play, interlinked and mutually dependent, without losing verisimilitude. It is only when the play is over and one looks back on it that the true theme— loyalty, or more properly, the inadequacy of loyalty —is made clear. The play stands firmly on its feet as a drama, rather thrilling, vivid, and at times moving; it would have made its appeal as "a slice of life" even if no moral had been implicit.

But it is superfluous to expatiate further on Galsworthy's uncommon talent for achieving fidelity to the outward-seeming of daily life, while manipulating his characters to express the inward moral in whose behalf he breaks a lance.

If the characters in the plays are, as it were, created whole, fixed in their essentials for all eternity, it is quite otherwise with the characters in the novels, from whose embryonic beginnings only their creator, if he, could have foretold their subsequent development and ends. The supreme example of this is, of

133

course, Soames, whose growth is chronicled so imperceptibly and yet so surely that we accept the likeable old man of *Swan Song* unquestioningly, and almost forget that in the first book of the Saga he seemed to be compounded of nothing but objectionable traits. But Soames is only one of many. The growth of Old Jolyon and Young Jolyon, of the Aunts many and various, of June, of Fleur, and many others of the Forsyte clan, is only less noteworthy than that of Soames because it plays a less prominent part in the scheme of the work. Only Irene remains, as of intention, remote, a lovely abstraction, seen through the eyes of those who love beauty, never through the eyes of the author, and never directly placed before the reader. I do not feel, as some critics do, that Irene is unreal: only that I have never met her face to face. Most of the Forsytes I seem to have known; Irene I have only heard about. It was this effect, I fancy, that Galsworthy wished to produce; for Irene was the only character in the whole of the half-score of volumes who could be held as a symbol, "a concretion of disturbing Beauty impinging on a possessive world," always remote and impalpable. For the rest, the Galsworthy world has little use for symbols. It is thickly peopled with human beings, some of them approximating to types, some of them vitally themselves, a few of them something less than alive.

In the last class—a small one—I should place some of his poor folk, who, seen from without and from a position rather distorted by pity, are sometimes less real men and women than the shadows of men and women. This is not, by any means, always the case. Old Westminster, in *Fraternity*, is real enough; Tryst in *The Freelands* is real enough, and real, too, are the lightly-touched-on characters who serve a subsidiary function, such as the policeman in *Saint's Progress*. It is when they play an important role—Bicket in *The White Monkey* springs to my mind—that his poor folk tend to be two-dimensional, lacking substance and roots. It is as if Galsworthy were interested in them as "the poor" rather than as human beings with as interesting a set of complexes as their betters'.

But if the so-called lower classes eluded Galsworthy, he seems to have had the freedom of most other strata of English society—professional, yeoman, patrician—all of which he populates with vital characters, some indeed whose vitality is their only saving grace. He was particularly happy in his old ladies. They rise before me numerously as I write. Frances Fleeming Freeland, that spirit strangely compounded of domination and humility, of acceptation and cynicism; precise and actual to the point of desert dryness, generous to a degree which caused her family to despair; and always, beyond all things, brave . . . with her little bottles of lotions and ointments, lozenges and plasters, new and unworkable but plausible gadgets, which she always seemed to carry on her person, ready to supply the needy with or without their consent. Aunt Em, one of Galsworthy's latest and most attractive creations, with her significant irrelevancies and shrewd inconsequence—impossible to describe or classify her! Her vitality can only be appreciated by savouring it in its context. Perhaps of all his women Margery Pendyce, in *The Country House*, has the most abiding charm. Delicate, gentle, with more imagination than her class is willing to sanction, she is the real heroine of *The Country House*; the property, by law, of her husband Horace Pendyce; the property, by love, of her son George, for whose sake she leaves her husband, returning to him later because she discovers that her love for her son gives her no claim to him, and because her husband, whom she had never loved, needs her; and perhaps because the custom of the country —that weighty, wingless creature born of time and of the earth—had its limbs fast twined around her. It had made her its mistress, and was not going to let her go. Margery Pendyce, something of a snob, always a lady, has a fragrancy which pervades the whole of the book.

The value of Galsworthy's work as a document, as an undistorting mirror of his times, is not likely to be denied. It is almost the only thing he claimed for it, and the appraising literary world, always ready to accept a cue which will lighten its labours, is perhaps too prone to estimate Galsworthy's achievement by his own modest claim. That he pictured certain upper sections of English society, from the latter half of the nineteenth century until the year of Grace 1932, more exactly, more fairly, more understandingly, more comprehensively, more delicately and more sympathetically than any other writer of his generation is patent. What does not seem to be so readily admitted is that it is impossible to draw a convincing picture of a society without peopling it copiously with vital characters. A vast collection of classifiable types might afford material for a bluebook: it would make a poor showing in a work of fiction whose immediate purpose was to reveal the growth of a family. The one certain attribute of a type is that it is fixed, even in the character of its growth, and leaves nothing to hazard. That the characters in the Forsyte books grow so naturally that wiseacres, wise only after the event, are persuaded that they can detect the formula of their growth, does not account for the immense success of the novels with the ordinary reading public, a public which does not read the critical reviews, but has certain touchstones of its own by which it judges the books it reads. Briefly, the great reading public demands (a) an entertaining story and (b) characters in which it can believe and be interested. This public was as familiar with the family history of the Forsytes as with its own; and I—not ignorant of Galsworthy's work—have been shamed by the knowledge of all the details of it revealed by subscribers to lending libraries who know not "The London Mercury."

VERSE

When Galsworthy first published his poems he called them "moods, songs and doggerels," which is an indication that he did not take them too seriously, and certainly laid no claims to great technical achievement. Many novelists find themselves worried by ideas which have no rightful place in a novel and yet claim artistic utterance; moods which clamour for concrete form and emotions which call for direct expression. The short poem is the most appropriate medium for the satisfaction of such needs and Galsworthy from time to time availed himself of it. His verse is unpretentious: it does not, as a rule, attempt to scale great heights in content, nor to tackle very formidable problems in technique. I have no doubt that he was a greater poet when he wrote prose than when he wrote verse, that his mastery of language was more justly shown by his novels than by his poems, and that his subtle perception was hampered rather than helped by the necessity to keep to the rhythm and rhyming of the verse-form. There are instances of awkward phrasing, arbitrary inversions, and words born of rhyme rather than sense, which he would not have tolerated in his prose works. Nevertheless, among his fifty poems there are a number which would have been worth preserving even if he had not attained fame in other fields. There is vigour and point in the poem called *Errantry* from which I have already quoted (page 55), and there is beauty in the poem *Dedication*, the aptness of which will be recognised by all who know the delicate and gracious lady, his wife, to whom it is inscribed:

> Thine is the solitude that rare flowers know,
> Whose face is slender aristocracy.
> And yet, of all that in the garden grow,
> None other has such sweet supremacy.
> For thine's the oldest secret of the world:
> How to be loved, and still to keep apart—
> A lily blown, a bud not yet uncurled—
> Gold-fortuned I, whose very breath thou art!

With great economy of words, too, he is able to call up a scene and express an idea, the dramatist assisting him in this. The poet looks at an empty house where his love once lived:

> From windows gaily lit,
> Where once in curtained dark
> My heaven used to hide,
> The memories wan and stark
> Troop down to me outside. (*Let*)

The same faculty is at work in *The Moon at Dawn*, in which the moon plays the unexpected role of harlot:

I saw her once, the insatiate moon,
Go stealing, coiffed with orange hood,
From night, her lover, still in swoon—
All wicked she, who once was good!

and *Straw in the Street* and *The Moor Grave* exploit a
similar gift of quick dramatic expression. Nature,
needless to say, is evoked in many poems with many
verbal felicities. The brief apostrophe to *The Downs*;
the neatly-drawn *Silver Point*, and *Autumn by the Sea*
offer examples; and there is a poem that is pure
Galsworthy, *Promenade*, from which I must quote a
few lines:

All sweet and startled gravity
My Love comes walking from the Park;
Her eyes are full of what they've seen—
The little bushes puffing green,
The candles pale that light the chestnut tree.

Only once did he break into free verse, in the poem
To Beauty quoted elsewhere. This is so immediate an
expression of his faith and needs that among the
many regrets which his premature passing leaves
with me is the regret that he did not live to develop
the gift of writing verse untrammelled by the rhyming which cramped his impulse.

HUMOUR

Galsworthy was not a wit, but his conversation
was freely sprinkled with a gentle humour and he was
readily responsive to wit and humour in others. His
own humour manifested itself more in a certain
whimsical turn of thought and expression than in
utterances which could be singled out, labelled

amusing, and quoted. The humorous aphorism was not one of his assets and he never laboured to scintillate. There is no doubt that his work is reputed in some circles to lack humour, and this delusion may be in part traceable to the fact that his public was curiously divided into those who knew him primarily as a playwright and those who knew him primarily as a novelist, and the two publics do not overlap as much as might be imagined. It is from the first of these divisions that the report of his lack of humour emanates, and the theatre-going public is, of course, much more vocal than the novel-reading public. Now, although there is plenty of humour in the plays, it is a fact that only one of them—*The Little Man*—is predominantly humorous; the comedy element does not dominate any of the others, and Galsworthy's most popular plays are, strangely enough, those which are most serious in purpose and the least lightened by humour—*Strife*, *Justice*, *The Skin Game*, *Loyalties*, *Escape* (in which there is a larger portion) and *The Silver Box*—an answer, by the way, to the managerial dogma that the public does not want serious plays.

One book, profoundly earnest in intention, is very consciously, a little too consciously, humorous in expression—*The Burning Spear*. For the rest, Galsworthy's novels are, like life, compounded of many elements of which humour is not the least. It is in his acute observation of character that his sense of humour is perhaps most apparent, and humorous commentary is one of the means by which he builds up a personality. His is rarely the kind of humour which makes one laugh aloud; aching ribs are not his goal, but every reader of the novels must be aware of the innumerable instances—not irrelevantly tacked on but integral—which have provoked the inward smile or the outward chuckle.

How perfectly the attitude of old Swithin Forsyte to the lovely Irene is shown by telling us that the expression like that of a cat who is just going to purr stole over his face: Mrs. Soames! . . . A pretty woman—and sympathetic to him! And the transferred epithet, "shy," in describing Aunt Juley's raiment, how revealing! She was sombrely magnificent this evening in black bombazine, with a mauve front cut in a shy triangle. It is in such tiny unforced details that the humorous flavour of Galsworthy's work is best shown, conversational, as it were, but selective. "A gentleman, old, and *by his hat* a professor of horticulture, passed . . ." "Bealby entered presently, preceded by his nose . . ."

Incidents are never introduced for the sake of humour, but always with the express purpose of forwarding the story or illuminating a character or a relationship. The memory which comes to lonely old Soames as he drives home one night is amusing, but it is significant also for the light it throws on his present and past, explaining his failure and evoking sympathy for his tragic incapacity to excite love. He remembers his first day at school— a brand-new little boy in a brand-new little top-hat, with a play box stored by his mother with things to eat, and blessed with the words: "There, Summy dear, that'll make you popular." He had reckoned on having command of that corruption for some weeks; but no sooner had he produced a bit of it, than they had taken the box, and suggested to him that it would be a good thing to eat the lot. In twenty-two minutes twenty-two boys had materially increased their weight, and he himself in handing out the contents, had been obliged to eat less than a twenty-third. They had left him one packet of biscuits, and those had caraway seeds, for which he had constitutionally no passion whatever. Afterwards three other new boys had complained that he was a fool for having eaten it all up like that, instead of saving it for them, and he had been obliged to sit on their heads one by one. His popularity had lasted twenty-two minutes, and, so far as he knew, had never come back. He had been against Communism ever since.

Leave out, or cut out, everything that is not to the point; leave in nothing that is not positively relevant —this is an axiom with Galsworthy and explains the drum-like tightness of his construction. The method might be likened to the method of classical music: no note must be left in which does not serve the whole structure. Ornament which is not implicit is superfluous. Soames walked through a narrow bit of wood where rooks were in a state of some excitement. He knew little about the habits of birds, not being detached enough from self for the study of creatures unconnected with him; but he supposed they would be holding a palaver about food—worm-currency would be depressed, or there had been some inflation or other—fussy as the French over their wretched franc. From this apparent digression we learn something more about Soames's incapacity to open out, about his instinctive association of everything with property, and his basic lack of sympathy with his French wife Annette.

Irony is implicit in the bulk of Galsworthy's work, sometimes flavoured with bitterness and sometimes with humour. Baynes was knighted when he built that public Museum of Art which has given so much

CRAFTSMAN

employment to officials, and so little pleasure to those working classes for whom it was designed. . . . The Forsytes collected pictures, too, and were supporters of such charitable institutions as might be beneficial to their sick domestics . . . Some of them paid for pews, thus expressing in the most practical form their sympathy with the teachings of Christ.

"Society has an excellent eye for the helpless; it never treads on people unless they're really down," says Ferrand in *The Island Pharisees*; and in the same book, in the author's own words: "An expression which, if he had not been a baronet, would have been a leer, came on his lips." What concentrated ironical comment in this bird's-eye view of the Pendyces (*Country House*): Had he been born a year before his brother, instead of a year after, Charles Pendyce would naturally have owned Worsted Skeynes, and Horace would have gone into the Army instead. As it was, having almost imperceptibly become a Major-General, he had retired, taking with him his pension. The third brother, had he chosen to be born, would have gone into the Church, where a living awaited him. . . . Tradition, privilege, class— pickled in a couple of sentences. The Reverend Hussell Barter, having passed at Oxford through certain examinations, had been certified at the age of twenty-four as a man fitted to impart to persons of both sexes rules of life and conduct after which they had been groping for twice or thrice that number of years . . .

Mrs. Barthwick's utterances (*Silver Box*) offer many examples of fatuousness and unconscious humour which I have quoted earlier.

Remembering the gait of girls who clung to fashion in the first few years after the war, the little dialogue between Michael Mont and his secretary is not uninstructive. Why, he asked, do modern girls walk in a curve, with their heads poked forward? They could not all be built like that. After some hesitation he elicited an explanation. "They aren't supposed to have anything be—behind, and, of course, they have, and they can't get the proper effect unless they curve their chests in and poke their heads forward."

Could a board-room be more aptly conveyed than by the description: "The room seemed to him to have been got by a concert-hall out of a station waiting-room." Atmosphere is created, too, by a haddock that was endeavouring to be fresh; and the innate snobbery of Cecilia Dallison is somehow emphasised by the knowledge that the complexion of a joint of roast beef reminded her uncomfortably of cabmen. How vividly one sees that small fair woman in the mean street, with a high, bald forehead, from which the hair was "gleaned" into curl-papers; and that cornucopia of a woman with an avid blue stare.

Certain privileged readers of this book will not fail to appreciate the humour of the statement that Stephen Dallison, when unable to get his golf on Saturdays, went to his club, and read the reviews. The two forms of exercise, in fact, were very similar; in playing golf you went round and round; in reading reviews you did the same, for in course of time you were assured of coming to articles that nullified articles already read.

More deliberately comical is the description of that mosquito hunt in which Colonel Ercott engaged before retiring to rest in the hotel Le Coeur d'or (*The Dark Flower*), forerunner to the similar chase in *The Roof*, but even here the opportunity of adding a further spot of light on character is not missed. The fact that other people did not so secure their windows did not at all trouble the Colonel, a true Englishman, who loved to act in his own way, and to think in the ways of other people . . . They would wait till night came, then burn a peculiar little lamp with a peculiar little smell, and, in the full glare of the gaslight, stand about on chairs, with slippers, and their eyes fixed on true or imaginary beasts. Then would fall little slaps, making little messes, and little joyous or doleful cries would arise.

The Burning Spear is a satire on war-time psychology and is Galsworthy's most sustained attempt at humour. The satire is telling and there is considerable fertility of idea, both in the characterisation and in the incidents designed to show how topsy-turvy human values become when fear is in possession. The humour verges on farce, and unlike most of Galsworthy's, is deliberately invented rather than born of character and circumstance, and appears therefore to be somewhat laboured. There is, however, much charm in the engaging figure of Lavender, a small thin gentleman of fifty-eight, gentle disposition, and independent means, whose wits had become somewhat addled from reading the writings and speeches of public men. A mixture of Don Quixote and Pickwick, dubbed Don Pickwixote by the V.A.D. Leonora who becomes his Dulcinea, he sets out to do his bit to save England and has many fantastic and significant adventures. Blink, his sheep dog, like all the Galsworthy animals, has a distinct personality—that mixture of stupidity and sagacity typical of the breed—and provides many amusing pages. But it would be invidious to detach specimens of humour from a book primarily humorous.

SEX

SEX

Of all the illusions which cling to the reputation of Galsworthy none is less justified than that which accuses him of being sex-shy. It is often assumed that his reticence in matters sexual was so extreme and Victorian that it verged on furtiveness. Those who find his work in general antipathetic are quick to discover that his treatment of sex is hypocritical, and, blind to the innumerable evidences to the contrary, they assume that his avoidance of the subject leads to those unhealthy symptoms which are produced by suppressions.

Nothing so significantly marks the changes in the mentality of a people as its attitude to sex. The freedom of the Elizabethans, the flowering expansiveness of their art and life, their recognition of the dignity of man; the coarseness of the Restoration, when smut and phosphorescent artificiality went side by side; the repressed and priggish Victorian Era, when smugness was almost synonymous with worthiness, have led by easy stages to a post-war England where psycho-analysis, generally misunderstood, has taken the place of religion, and its jargon, generally misapplied, is on the lips of all who have reached puberty. The findings of such eminent psychologists as Freud, Jung, Adler, Groddeck cannot be lightly passed over; they are deeply interesting and important, but they are still tentative, mutually contradictory and inconclusive, and it will be many years before it would be safe to base a scheme of conduct or education upon them. But even if the complexes, libidos, fixations, inhibitions, suppressions, adaptations, and the whole bag o' tricks had been definitely taped, sealed and branded with ungainsayable truth, they would be of no more use to the artist, as a tool in his workshop, than the discoveries of Einstein, Eddington, Jeans, Bertram Thomas or Leonard Woolley. They would enrich his mind, possibly disturb his convictions and stimulate his thought and emotions, and in that way influence his work as an artist. But the moment a writer looks outside himself for help in the development of a character born of his own creative impulse, he is lost. The certitude of the artist yields place to the scepticism of the scientist, and characters which had life given them by a convinced parenthood become robots constructed to a formula.

D. H. Lawrence was an example of this. The characters in his earlier books—most of all in that masterpiece *Sons and Lovers*—live with a vitality incomparably greater than that which informs the characters of later works. In *Sons and Lovers*, Lawrence, relying solely on his instincts as an artist, allowed his people to act according to the laws inherent in their own being; that their behaviour in many respects accorded with the theories of Freud before Freud was even a name in this country, is a tribute to the truth of Lawrence's inspiration and to the insight and skill of Freud as a psychologist. I do not know when Freud and his co-workers first burst upon Lawrence, but it is sufficiently obvious that in proportion as he became absorbed in what may be roughly classed as psycho-analysis, so did his characters become less individuals, standing upright and self dependent, and more a concretion of abstract formulae.

SEX

It is not out of caprice that I have dragged the name of Lawrence into a study of Galsworthy. The latter, as far as I know, had never publicly expressed an opinion of Lawrence, the man or his work, and at the moment I can recall only one occasion when he referred to him at all. It was when I showed him a message which Lawrence sent to the P.E.N. in March 1929:

"All my good wishes to the P.E.N.," he wrote. "Even if I'm the black sheep amongst its members, yet I feel that wherever I go P.E.N. would accept me and be kind to me if I'd let them—all over the face of the earth—which is somehow comforting."

Handing the note back to me, Galsworthy said: "That's nice of him."

Lawrence on Galsworthy was more loquacious. In 1928 he issued a peculiarly venomous attack,* written in that strange rambling, uncontrolled style which so often disfigured his later work. The occasional gleam of illuminating commentary is almost quenched by the torrent of abuse, inexactitudes, and wilful misunderstanding and by that meaningless repetition which seems to indicate a need to convince himself of the truth of his charges. This is not the place to set up a defence of Galsworthy against the attacks of Lawrence. Lawrence is, alas, gone and could not answer back, and already posterity has begun the winnowing process which will finally determine how much or how little of his work and of Galsworthy's is mete for survival. But as Lawrence, who was apt to claim a monopoly in sexual knowledge, has pronounced judgement on this aspect of Galsworthy's work, and his view is representative

*"Scrutinies." Collected by Edgell Rickword. Wishart & Co.

of a certain section of public opinion, it is worth
while citing the salient features of the attack and
seeing to what extent they are justified.

"We look at this love, this PASSION," he writes, "and
we see nothing but a doggish amorousness and a sort
of anti-Forsyteism. They are the *anti* half of the
show. Runaway dogs of these Forsytes, running in
the back garden and furtively and ignominiously
copulating—this is the effect on me, of Mr. Galsworthy's grand love affairs, Dark Flowers or Bosin-
neys, or Apple Trees or George Pendyces—whatever
they be. About every one of them something ig-
nominious and doggish, like dogs copulating in the
street, and looking round to see if the Forsytes are
watching. . . .

"Bosinney is a property hound, but he has run
away from the kennels, or been born outside the
kennels, so he is a rebel. So he goes sniffing round
the property bitches, to get even with the successful
property hounds that way . . .

"Irene seems to me a sneaking, creeping, spiteful
sort of bitch, an anti-Forsyte, absolutely living off the
Forsytes—yes, to the very end; absolutely living off
their money and trying to do them dirt. She is like
Bosinney, a property mongrel doing dirt in the
property kennels . . ." and so on.

"It is when he comes to sex that Mr. Galsworthy
collapses finally. He becomes nastily sentimental.
He wants to make sex important, and he only makes
it repulsive . . ." and so on.

"Anything of the real meaning of sex, which in-
volves the whole human being, never occurs to him
(i.e., Shelton in *The Island Pharisees*). It is a function
and the female is a sort of sexual appliance, no more.
And so we have it again and again, on this low and

bastard level, all the human correspondence lacking. The sexual level is extraordinarily low, like dogs. The Galsworthy heroes are all weirdly in love with themselves, when we know them better, afflicted with chronic narciscism. They know just three types of women: the Pendyce mother, prostitute to property; the Irene, the essential *anti* prostitute, the floating, flaunting female organ; and the social woman, the mere lady."

And so the attack proceeds, repeating the same ideas, slightly varied in phraseology, with the same metaphors and comparisons—dogs and bitches and the attributes of dogs and bitches, and on, over and over again, until one is nauseated by contact with a mind apparently incapable of seeing anything save through the haze arising from its own sexual and cloacal obsessions.

"THE BEAUTY AND LOVING IN THE WORLD. . . ."

If it were admitted that Lawrence's view of Galsworthy's treatment of sex was just, it would be tantamount to confessing that Galsworthy had failed as a novelist, since the mainspring of human action is love in its infinite manifestations, and a novelist who was incapable of seeing it truly and whole, neither shirking facts nor sentimentalising them, would be lacking in the essential equipment of his art. To ignore sex, to under-estimate its importance, to falsify its phenomena in order to ingratiate a sentimental public, would be a cardinal sin—a greater betrayal of the novelist's privileges, even, than the over-emphasis of one aspect of sex, the purely physical, which was Lawrence's own sin against the Holy Ghost.

Galsworthy has touched on sexual love from almost
every conceivable angle, but has never deemed it
necessary to underline or describe those physical
details which are so alluring to the more advanced
of our latter-day novelists. His reticence in this
matter was deliberate, not simply the following of the
line of least resistance. He was familiar with such
detailed outpourings as the last chapter of Mr.
Joyce's *Ulysses*, but had no wish to emulate them. I
recall the novel which Michael Mont (*The White
Monkey*) was reading that was all about a man who,
when he was a boy, had been so greatly impressed
by the sight of a maid-servant changing her clothes
in a room over the way, that his married life was a
continual struggle not to be unfaithful with his wife's
maid. Michael only got as far as that in the manuscript; he decided that the rest of the book would
doubtless show how the complex was resolved, going
most conscientiously into all those precise bodily
details which it was now so timorous and Victorian
to leave out. "Genuine piece of work," is Michael's
comment on it, "and waste of time to go on with it."
And that would have been Galsworthy's own point
of view.

The importance with which Galsworthy invested
sex is shown by his preoccupation with the tragic
consequences of ill-matched unions. Does he not say
in the preface to *The Forsyte Saga* itself that the simple
truth underlying the whole story is that where sex
attraction is utterly and definitely lacking in one
partner to a union, no amount of pity, or reason, or
duty, or what not, can overcome a repulsion implicit in Nature. Whether it ought to, or no, is beside
the point; because in fact it never does. The hatred
underlying the sexual intimacy of two ill-assorted

creatures is referred to so far back in Galsworthy's career as the early pages of *The Island Pharisees*, linked up, as ever, with the instinct for possession which is one of the dominating features of modern civilisation; and *The Country House* contains many variations on the same theme. Gregory is overwhelmed by the thought that the woman whom he loves is wedded to a man whom she despises and he inveighs against the law of the land which makes unlinking almost impossible. He envisioned her in the coils of a great slimy serpent, and the knowledge that each man and woman unhappily married was, whether by his own, his partner's, or by no fault at all, in the same embrace, afforded him no comfort whatsoever.

Almost more devastating is the bleakness of the married life of Hilary and Bianca (*Fraternity*)—Bianca the victim, like Soames, of the uncontrollable tragedy of being unlovable, and Hilary, delicate to a fault, introverted, pressed in more and more on himself, till his instincts are atrophied and his very personality warped. Public sentiment is always in advance of the law, and public sentiment would certainly favour greater ease in the severing of bonds which inflict needless suffering. Courtier in *The Patrician*, in which the theme is once more dwelt on, is convincingly emphatic in condemning the law of divorce: "When this law, by enforcing spiritual adultery on those who have come to hate their mates, destroys the sanctity of the married state, the very sanctity it professes to uphold, you must expect to have it broken by reasoning men and women without their losing self-respect."

Whatever the theme of the book or the play— law, industrial strife, the possessive instinct, the land, the decay of aristocratic society, the incongruity of religious orthodoxy in the modern world—it is love, sexual love, which runs like a connecting thread through the whole of Galsworthy's work, providing the motive force and infinitely the deepest share of the emotional content. Married love, "illicit" love, young love, unrequited love, tormented and satisfied love—all phases of love seem to have a place in his scheme.

The poignancy and fragrancy of young love shine through many of his pages, expressed with as intimate an understanding when he was in his middle sixties as when he was thirty years younger. Holly and Val, Jon and Fleur, Nedda and Derek, Noel and Cyril, the young lovers in *The Roof*—innumerable instances come to mind, idylls of youthful love. One remembers when Fleur, in love for the only time, kisses Jon on the forehead, leaving a little cool place between the brows, like the imprint of a flower. Love filled his soul, that love of boy and girl which knows so little, hopes so much, would not brush the down off for the world, and must become in time a fragrant memory—a searing passion—a humdrum mateship —or, once in many times, a vintage full and sweet with sunset colour on the grapes.

There is an exquisite chapter in *The Freelands* in which Nedda, awakened to love for the first time pours out her heart into the secret keeping of her diary, written so convincingly that we feel that only so could a romantic but unsentimental girl like Nedda have expressed herself. And then there followed the later tormenting questionings: did he love her, could he love her, he so infinitely marvellous, she so unworthy? She must have dreamed it Dreamed that most wonderful, false dream. And the reassurance which came when Derek's arms were around her, and they sat on the stairs clinging together, comforting each other with hands and lips and whisperings. This love seems doomed to tragedy—the dark, tormented, mysterious nature of the boy forbodes disaster, and to the end one has misgivings. Nothing could be more delicate than Galsworthy's telling of this story, nor more subtle than his understanding of the inconsequent fancifulness of young lovers with some gift of self-expression; the heroics of the male and the delighted yielding of the female, the blossoming of beauty and joy, with a shadowy fear somewhere far away in the background.

"Derek, I feel like a hill with the sun on it!"

"I feel like that yellow cloud with the wind on it."

"I feel like an apple-tree coming into blossom."

"I feel like a giant."

"I feel like a song."

"I feel I could sing you."

"On a river, floating along."

"A wide one, with great plains on each side, and beasts coming down to drink, and either the sun or a yellow moon shining, and someone singing, too, far off."

The Bright Young Things of to-day express themselves differently, but Galsworthy was not writing of them. Before the Bright Young Things were, there was the Great War which gave them birth. During the war young people, adolescent or prematurely mature, had a difficult time. The inexorable course of nature was expected to be diverted and love held either in abeyance or handled so lightly that its roots remained superficial. Deep attachments were not

desirable in a world where young men were liable to
be swept away never to return. The shallower the
emotion, the quicker the recovery. Attachments
which were not taken too seriously received encour-
agement and Love and Religion were perhaps the
only fundamentals to which the principle, "Business
as Usual for the period of the War," did not apply.
Noel, daughter of the Reverend Edward Pierson,
(*Saint's Progress*) was altogether too deep for the
period in which she attained womanhood, but she
shared the general desire to get as much as possible
out of life lest it should be snatched from her. Convinced that her love for Cyril was the real thing, she
intended to have everything she could with him while
there was the chance. If marriage was forbidden,
there should at least be love. The coming together in
sexual love of Noel and Cyril could have been treated
in many ways. D. H. Lawrence would certainly have
imbued it with an exciting vitality so intense that the
sheer physicality of the relationship would have been
realised, and his almost mystical belief in the divinity
of the flesh would probably have endowed the situation with beauty. To every artist his own method.
Galsworthy, who would have subscribed to Brown-
ing's "All good things are ours, nor soul helps flesh
more, now, than flesh helps soul," makes the incident
vivid in his own way. It was night. Noel and Cyril
sat in the dark, and watched for the moon to come
up. They sat close together. Noel's face still had on it
that strange look of waiting; and Cyril sat obedient,
with his hand on her heart, and his own heart beating almost to suffocation. They sat, still as mice, and
the moon crept up. It laid a first vague greyness on
the high wall, which spread slowly down and bright-
ened till the lichen and the grasses up there were

visible; then crept on, silvering the dark above their heads. Noel pulled his sleeve, and whispered: "See!" There came the white owl, soft as a snow-flake, drifting across in that unearthly light, as if flying to the moon. And just then the top of the moon itself looked over the wall, a shaving of silvery gold. It grew, became a bright spread fan, then balanced there, full and round, the colour of pale honey. "Ours!" Noel whispered.

No more.

The story which follows the birth of Noel's illegiti-mate baby begotten by her dead soldier lover under the pale moon, is as poignant as anything Galsworthy ever wrote, and her grief in the loss of her man is com-parable to Dinny's in *Flowering Wilderness*, when, abandoned by her lover Wilfrid Desert, she goes home, like a wounded animal, knowing that, unlike an animal, who makes no pretence of keeping up appearances, she must watch every word and look, must smile and smile, and show nothing. The hay was still lying out in the field attached to her home and she flung herself down. She wanted desperately these few minutes of abandonment. She didn't cry, but pressed herself against the hay-covered earth, and the sun burned her neck. She turned on her back and gazed up at the blue. She framed no thoughts, dis-solved in aching for what was lost and could never be found now. And the hum of summer beat drowsily above her from the wings of insects drunk on heat and honey. She crossed her arms on her chest to compress the pain within her. If she could die, there, now, in full summer with its hum and singing of the larks; die and ache no more! So she lay motionless, until the dog came and licked her cheeks. And, ashamed, she got up and stood brushing the hay-seeds and stalks from her dress and stockings.

Sexual attraction that has little to identify it with altruistic love is a recurring motive in Galsworthy's work. Sometimes it is used as a conscious device, the "sexual appeal" of the modern cliché; sometimes it is an involuntary emanation which brings disaster on itself and others. All that is tragic in the life of Soames's first wife, Irene, springs largely from the unwitting exercise of a power to disturb the senses of men and make them desire her. It was this which made Soames swear a score of times that if their marriage was not a success, she should be as free as if she had never married him—a promise forgotten within a few days of the making of it. It was this which made him commit the unforgivable crime of forcibly asserting his marital rights; it was this which, when he knew that Bosinney had been Irene's lover, made him suppress a desire to say melodramatically "take your hated body, that I love, out of my house. Take away that pitiful white face, so cruel and soft, before I crush it. Get out of my sight; never let me see you again" and, eating humble pie, bid her remain in his house. It was this which caused him to pocket his pride again years later, long after they had separated, and sent him back to her with a plea to let bygones be bygones. "Is it unnatural to want a child from one's own wife?" he asks. "I want you back. I want you."

A problem almost identical with that of Irene is that of Clare in *The Fugitive*. Sexual incompatibility so extreme that she can only think of her marriage as the reconciliation of two animals, one of them unwilling. She too has that sort of beauty which acts as an

Photo: Walter Benington.

IRENE ROOKE IN "THE FUGITIVE."

To face p. 160.

irritant to what are called men's animal passions;
she, like Irene, made a bad bargain and is unable to
carry it out. Her husband, like Irene's, is pitiable
rather than objectionable; his chief failing is a lack
of imagination, for which he cannot be held responsible, and a belief in the false gods of Respectability
and Appearances which will not sanction the release
of his lawful wife from a bondage which has become
unendurable.

"Do you suppose we're the only couple who've
found things aren't what they thought, and have to
put up with each other and make the best of it?"
he asks. And "Not by thousands," is Clare's bitter
reply, revealing Galsworthy's conviction.

Irene, a concretion of disturbing Beauty impinging
on a possessive world, is only secondarily an embodiment of sex attraction. Several other characters in
the novels and the plays seem to play practically no
other role. There is the little model in *Fraternity*. A
pariah, a young girl without property or friends,
spiritually soft, physically alluring, who, with simple
devotion, laid siege to Hilary; tried to weave a spell
over him with her mute, stubborn adoration, inviting
him in some strange unconscious, subtle way to treat
her as a woman, as though in spirit she had linked
her round young arms about his neck, and through
her half-closed lips were whispering the eternal call
of sex to sex.

A similar character is Victorine, the girl in *The
White Monkey* who sacrifices her own sense of propriety by sitting as a model in the "altogether" that
she might earn enough money to pay the passage of
herself and her seedy husband to Australia. She, too,
a girl of the people, had that strangely alluring
beauty which disturbed men's senses. Mona-Lisa-

ish, sallow, large-eyed, dead-black bobbed frizzy-ended hair—Aubrey Green, for whom she posed in *L'après midi d'une Dryade*, seemed to take some credit to himself for not having seduced her.

Another item in this picture gallery of humble but tragic beauties is the nineteen-year-old Megan in *The Pigeon*, outcast but invested with the fatal allure that makes the Belgian Ferrand toy with her hand within half an hour of meeting her. It is probably not without design that she, too, serves as a painter's model, as if to emphasise Galsworthy's belief that man, beholding Beauty, cannot resist the temptation to seize it and transfix it, like a butterfly caught in flight.

Love and Beauty and Sex, as theme and counter-theme, linked or identified, permeate Galsworthy's work, and even Edward Pierson, the saint whose progress ends in the Calvary of disillusionment, remembers with uneasiness a remark made by his doctor son-in-law—"Love of beauty is really only the sex instinct, which nothing but complete union satisfies." The beauty which is love comes to men in a vision, as it came to George Pendyce when he met Helen Bellew, another of Galsworthy's curiously remote women, whose beauty stimulates, distracts, and leaves unsatisfied. To some men that vision comes but once, to some men many times. It comes after long winter, when the blossom hangs; it comes after parched summer, when the leaves are going gold; and of what hues it is painted—of frost-white and fire, of wine and purple, of mountain flowers, or the shadowy green of still deep pools—the seer alone can tell. But this is certain—the vision steals from him who looks on it all images of other things, all sense of law, of order, of the living past and the living present. It is the future, fair-scented, singing, jewelled, as when suddenly between high banks a bough of apple-blossom hangs quivering in the winds loud with the song of bees.

Even superficial acquaintance with the novels would evoke many pictures of lovers—nameless lovers of whom the principal characters become aware through the intensity of their own longings and frustrations. Through their eyes we see them. Gregory (*The Country House*), idealist to the point of fanaticism, stricken by the sense of his own hopeless love, walked towards the Park, suffering from black loneliness; and he lay first on his face, and then on his back, with his hand always over his eyes. And around him were other men lying on the grass, and some were lonely, and some hungry, and some asleep, and some were lying there for the pleasure of doing nothing and for the sake of the hot sun on their cheeks; and by the side of some lay their girls, and it was these that Gregory could not bear to see, for his spirit and his senses were a-hungered. In the plantations close by were pigeons, and never for a moment did they stop their cooing; never did the blackbirds cease their courting songs; the sun its hot, sweet burning; the clouds above their love-chase in the sky. It was the day without a past, without a future, when it was not good for a man to be alone. And no man looked at him, because it was no man's business.

It was in Hyde Park, too, that Bianca (*Fraternity*) wandered, Bianca the victim of a temperament which awakened no man to love, into a grove of trees which had almost eluded the notice of the crowd. They were limes, guarding still within them their honey bloom. Their branches of light, broad leaves, near heart-shaped, were spread out like wide skirts. The tallest of these trees, a beautiful, gay creature, stood tremulous, like a mistress waiting for her tardy lover. What joy she seemed to promise, what delicate enticement, with every veined quivering leaf. And suddenly the sun caught hold of her, raised her up to him, kissed her all over; she gave forth a sigh of happiness, as though her very spirit had travelled through her lips up to her lover's heart.

The "pathetic fallacy," as Ruskin called it, of endowing nature with the emotion which one is experiencing oneself, is often an effective instrument in Galsworthy's hands, and this is only one of many examples of its use. Bianca passed on, observing the clandestine meeting of a pair of lovers, the intimacy of parading couples, and presently she saw a little boy and girl asleep on the doorstep of a mansion, with their cheeks pressed close together and their arms round each other, and again she hurried on.

Couples lingering on benches along the river bank, couples quietly engrossed in each other as they take their walks abroad, couples blotted against trees or on the grass, darker than the darkness, very silent, couples sitting cheek by jowl for an hour of idle Elysium snatched from the monotony of their treadmill; the couple whom Soames saw from the rise overlooking the Serpentine, in full lamp-light, black against the silver water, the woman's face buried in the man's neck—a single form, like a carved emblem of passion, silent and unashamed . . . they people the interstices of all Galsworthy's works, as if to declare that without love there is nothing. Labour and accumulate, add to your possessions, fret and fume about your duty to God and man, tyrannise over others, mortify yourself, glorify your country— but unless you have the power of identifying yourself unselfishly with another human being you are, in this world at any rate, doomed to unhappiness.

"*THE DARK FLOWER OF PASSION* . . ."

The dark flower of forbidden passion blooms abundantly in the Galsworthy world. Mark Lennan, of *The Dark Flower*, is not the only victim of its irresistible attraction, but it is in that book that the theme finds its most exhaustive expression. As a boy, he awakens in a woman of thirty-six the passion and desire never stimulated by her husband. She struggles against it; it haunts her; she prays to be relieved of it (for she is devout); she tries to transmute it to an attitude of motherly altruistic affection, but, moved by primitive forces, she is unable to prevent herself from awakening in the boy the desire she craves for; and time, place, and circumstances—the night, the moon, music and the scent of flowers—work together . . . and he feels her lips press his mouth with a swift burning kiss. An emotion is born, only half-real, a period of torment begun, his nature deepened . . . and the woman passes out of his life. Time passes and Mark Lennan, grown to young manhood, is again the victim of a love which fate condemns to unfulfilment. He brings to it all that naiveté, that touching quality of young Englishmen whose secret instinct it is to back away from the full nature of love, even from admitting that it has that nature. This time it is a married woman who inspires him, again a woman unsuitably mated. She had been sure that love would never come to her; had not wanted it—very much; had thought to go on well enough, and pass out at the end, never having known, or much cared to know, full summer. Love had taken its revenge on her now for all slighted love

offered her in the past. Now it had come to her, this
witchery, this dark sweet feeling, springing up, who
knew how or why? Her yielding to this love brought
no remorse. This was the meaning of Life. . . . As
well might grass stay its ripening because it shall be
cut down, as deny this call. Whatever power had
made her heart, had placed within it this love. But
whatever power had implanted this love in her heart
also decreed a tragic ending of it, and all Lennan's
determination that her life, in gratitude for love and
adoration she had bestowed upon him, should hold
nothing but joy, availed nothing.

And years later, now forty-six, Lennan, married
and loving his wife, is again swept off his feet by the
passionate devotion which a young girl, do what he
will to hold it at bay, lavishes upon him. The queer,
unhappy restlessness which not infrequently takes
possession of men in their middle years, assailed him;
a feeling that life was slipping, ebbing away within
reach of him, and his arms never stretched out to
arrest it . . . a feeling that no Englishman of forty-
six, in excellent health, ought for a moment to have
been troubled with. A feeling such as, indeed, no
Englishman ever admitted having—so that there was
not even, as yet, a society for its suppression. He
loved his wife; he and she had grown up as children
together; his allegiance was to her. But he was a
man, and his senses had been aroused. He ought to
have said: "No! You are a foolish child, and I an
elderly idiot!" But he had neither courage nor clear-
ness of mind enough; nor—the desire. Passion never
plays the game. Though it live but a day in the sun,
though it drown in tenebrous night, the dark flower
of passion will have its hour.

But—and this is a characteristic Galsworthy touch

—restraint, a sense of honour, loyalty and compassion are stronger even than his passion: he breaks with the girl before it is too late. His wife has triumphed. He ruminates over the fire. What memories a fire gathers into it, with its flaky ashes its little leaf-like flames, and that quiet glow and flicker! What tale of passions! How like to a fire was a man's heart! The first young fitful leapings, the sudden, fierce, mastering heat, the long, steady sober burning, and then—that last flaming-up, that clutch back at its own vanished youth, the final eager flight of flame, before the ashes wintered it to nothing. . . . Love! A strange haphazardous thing was love—so spun between ecstasy and torture! A thing insidious, irresponsible, desperate. A flying sweetness, more poignant than anything on earth, more dark in origin and destiny.

Broadly speaking, Galsworthy in his treatment of sex is prone to follow the main stream rather than to venture into those obscure bystreams which contribute to the great flow of sexual emotion somewhat loosely called love. Morbid psychology did not greatly interest him, and it is not perhaps irrelevant to recall that he told me once that although he recognised their significance and power, the great Scandinavian dramatists did not much attract him. Nevertheless, whether instinctively or because of his wide reading, there are innumerable unemphasised instances of an understanding of, or at least a familiarity with, some of the hidden springs of conduct, whose nature is enveloped in a darkness which even the psycho-analysts have only faintly illumined.

Any properly-equipped Bright Young Thing will rattle off a list of the complexes from which he or she or his or her friends are suffering, and will tell you with glib assurance that the reason why Ann finds Rodney so unsatisfactory is that he is still subconsciously in love with his mother, and that the proof of Eric's devotion to Elizabeth is the violence with which he attacks her. There is, often enough, an element of truth in these crude diagnoses, but such rough and ready psychology is of little use to the writer concerned with the subtle ramifications and growth of human character, in which motives are rarely unadulterated and actions only superficially the effect of their apparent causes.

Was Freud known even to professional psychologists in 1907 when *The Country House* appeared? Modern analysis would certainly have something to say of the relationship between Margery Pendyce and her son. Here we have another case of a wife who has made shift with a husband whom she does not really love and has concentrated all her affection on a son who has long since cut the apron-strings. When he is disowned, she decides, without anger or reproaches, to leave her husband. She goes to her son's club, and not finding him, asks leave to write a note. The porter shows her to a room with the quiet discretion of one who aids a mistress to her lover. And as she sits down at the table where probably George has sat to write to his mistress, using that very pen, Mrs. Pendyce's heart ached jealously. "Do come, soon, my dear. I shall be lonely and unhappy till I see you," she writes, and she signs herself "Your loving, Margery Pendyce." And this note, adds the author, which was just what she would have sent to a lover, took that form, perhaps unconsciously, because she had never had a lover thus to write to. And all that night, with one short interval of sleep, she ate of bitter isolation and futility, and of the still more bitter knowledge "George does not want me; I'm no good to him!" She had other children and she loved them too, but it was not the same thing, quite; she had never wanted them to want her, because that part of her had been given once for all to George. And when at last he came to her, broken, her heart was full of relief and shame and compassion, jealousy, love and deep longing. She watched his face, dearest to her in all the world, bent towards the flower, and she so yearned to hold it to her breast that, since she dared not, the tears stole up and silently rolled down her cheeks. . . . Presently, falling on her knees beside her son, she pulled his head down against her breast, and stayed rocking herself to and fro, silently shifting closer till she could feel his head lie comfortable; so, she had his face against her heart, and she could not bear to let it go. Her knees hurt her on the boarded floor, her back and all her body ached; but not for worlds would she relax an inch, believing that she could comfort him with her pain, and her tears fell on his neck. When at last he drew his face away she sank down on the floor, and could not rise, but her fingers felt that the bosom of her dress was wet.

Here is the perfect artistic embodiment—with many supporting details which are not quoted here —of a relationship which we should be justified in labelling Freudian, written before the word would have carried any significance in this country. There are many minor hints of instinctive Freudianism. The Reverend Hussell Barter entered his wife's room when she was in labour of yet another child and asked "Rose dear, Rose, can I do anything?" And Mrs. Barter murmured vaguely: "No, dear, nothing. Better go for your walk." But a gleam of malice shot into her eyes, hinting at the unadmitted antagonism which a woman feels for the man she does not love who has gratified his desire at the cost of her suffering.

The Groddeck belief that a man is always struggling with a desire to return to his mother's womb, is implicit in the picture of the poor child in *Fraternity*, whose little fists, and nose, and forehead, and even his little naked crinkled feet, were thrust with all his feeble strength against his mother's bosom, as though he were striving to creep into some hole away from life. There was a sort of dumb despair in that tiny pushing of his way back to the place whence he had come.

There is a suggestion, too, in the building-up of the widowed Pierson's character (*Saint's Progress*) that he is more than half in love with his daughter Noel. No one had told him in so many words that he should have married again—that to stay unmarried was bad for him, physically and spiritually, fogging and perverting life; not driving him, indeed as it drove many to intolerance and cruelty, but to that half-living dreaminess, and the vague unhappy yearnings which so constantly beset him. There is a sense of extraordinarily intimate love between him and Noel. Once when she flung her arms round him, he, half smothered by that fervent embrace, kissed her cheeks and hair. Freed of each other at last, he stood for a moment looking at her by the moonlight. "There never was anyone more loving than you, Nollie," he said quietly. "And good night, my love!" Then afraid to stay another second, he went quickly out of the dark little room.

The behaviour of Joy in the play which bears that

name is significant. Says Mrs. Hope: "She's more in love with her mother than anyone, follows her about like a dog!" Remember that *Joy* was produced in 1907.

June's passion for helping "lame dogs," concentrating all her emotional power on them and their needs, is the sublimated expression of the sexual energy which was dammed and thwarted by the loss of her lover, Bosinney. Sexual psychologists would not be slow to find the right category into which to place Gyp's Aunt Rosamund (*Beyond*). She was a tall, handsome woman, with a long, aristocratic face, deep-blue, rather shining eyes, a gentlemanly manner, warm heart, and a not unmelodious drawl. Very fond of Gyp, what passed within her mind as to their real relationship, remained very discreetly hidden. She was, too, something of a humanitarian, and the girl had just that softness which fascinates women who perhaps might have been happier if they had been born men. A cheery soul, given to long coats and waistcoats, stocks, and a crutch-handled stick. It is relevant to recall Gregory's casual remark in *The Country House*: "I hear all women intend to be men."

Do not let me read into such passages as these more than is there. All I would claim is that Galsworthy's responsiveness to the phenomena of human psychology was so accurate that, whether he knew it or not—and for my part I do not doubt his knowledge—he could not but embody in his work whatever of modern thinking accorded with his own sense of truth. In his last novel, *Over the River*, he shows himself aware of the candour with which the younger generation approaches sex and with their greater freedom both in speech and action. Acting as

JOHN GALSWORTHY

a mirror to this, he allows himself a certain license
which would have been incongruous in earlier books.
"The subtle difference which creeps into the charm
of a woman who has known physical love, and the
sting which the knowledge of that implants in a man's
senses" is an observation which would have struck a
discordant note in the earlier part of the *Forsyte Saga*,
for instance.

It seems appropriate to wind up this chapter with
a quotation from *Over the River*, Galsworthy's last
words, it might be said, on love. It is Adrian who
broods: "By love was man flung into the world;
with love was he in business nearly all his days,
making debts or profits; and when he died was by
the results of love, if not by the parish, buried and
forgotten. In this swarming London not a creature
but was deeply in account with a Force so whimsical, inexorable, and strong that none, man or
woman, in their proper senses would choose to do
business with it. 'Good match,' 'happy marriage,'
'ideal partnership,' 'just a flare up,' 'tragic state of
things,' 'misfit'! All his other activities man could
insure, modify, foresee, provide against (save the inconvenient activity of death); love he could not. It
stepped to him out of the night, into the night
returned. It stayed, it fled. On one side or the other
of the balance sheet it scored an entry, leaving him to
cast up and wait for the next entry. It mocked
dictators, parliaments, judges, bishops, police, and
even good intentions; it maddened with joy and
grief; wantoned, procreated, thieved and murdered;
was devoted, faithful, fickle. It had no shame, and
owned no master; built homes and gutted them;
passed by on the other side; and now and again
made of two hearts one heart till death."

"THE BEAUTY OF THE WORLD"

"THE BEAUTY OF THE WORLD"

"THE Beauty of the world is the novelist's real despair," wrote Galsworthy once: "the heartache that
he feels in the presence of Nature in flower."

The Galsworthy world was a beautiful world. He
let you accompany him to courts of law, prison cells,
solicitors' offices; would occasionally give you a
glimpse of slums darkling in the shadow of rich men's
houses, or call up a vision of a Victorian home heavy
with ugliness. But the physical world of which he
was most aware was a world of sheer beauty: he
loved it passionately and reverently and paid it
generous tribute. Dipping into the memory and
allowing the mind's eye to wander where it will in
Galsworthy's world, one goes from one scene of
enchantment to another, led by a poet. Nature,
in a hundred aspects, is revealed in grandeur and
intimacy, sometimes ministering comfort to man in
his distress, sometimes wounding him by her utter
detachment, and sometimes deriding him by running
counter to his mood. The author rarely speaks of
her in his own person, preferring to look at her
through the eyes of his characters, responding to her
through their senses, by this means the more vividly
evoking her.

I remember walking with him a year or two before
his death over the Sussex Downs. It was a grey,
windy afternoon: the previous day it had rained unceasingly and we had little hope of returning dry. The

inevitable dog accompanied us, but was left to pursue its own interests, which were many. We walked briskly; J.G., although in the middle sixties, was as vigorous as a young man. Pausing on a ridge above Bury, we looked out over the sweep of the Downs, silvery and remote, reserved and unspectacular, placid and curiously self-possessed. Not unlike Galsworthy himself, I thought.

"You wouldn't see that anywhere except in England," he said; and we tried to discover what it is about the Downs which so distinguishes them from all other hills and stamps them as peculiarly English.

"There's something clean, swept . . ." and he added, almost apologetically, "spiritual about them."

It was the right word, and although it had not come into my mind at the time, it is the one which—hesitating as he had done—I should have been inclined to apply to Galsworthy himself. Like many other good words, it has been hard-ridden of late and the edge of its meaning has become blurred, but using it to connote a fineness of fibre, a lack of material grossness, and a primary concern with things of the mind rather than of the body, it could have been applied to Galsworthy with perfect appositeness. And it was characteristic that he should have boggled at the word—it savoured of excess, and J. G. would always rather have under-stated than over-stated. The Downs unfolded before us in a series of gradually changing pictures as we continued our walk, in silence, or talking as the mood decided. I have seen many places with Galsworthy as a companion, more often abroad than in England, but it is the Downs which I always associate with him. His books have called up many scenes with which I seem almost as familiar as with those seen with my own eyes.

"On the spur of the Sussex Downs, inland from Nettlefold, stands a beech-grove. The traveller who enters it out of the heat and brightness, takes off the shoes of his spirit before its sanctity; and reaching the centre, across the clean beech-mat, he sits refreshing his brow with air, and silence. For the flowers of sunlight on the ground under those branches are pale and rare, no insects hum, the birds are almost mute. And close to the border trees are the quiet, milk-white sheep, in congregation, escaping from the noon heat. Here, above the fields and dwellings, above the ceaseless network of men's doings, and the vapour of their talk, the traveller feels solemnity. All seems conveying dignity—the great white clouds moving their wings above him, the faint longing murmur of the boughs, and in far distance, the sea. And for a space his restlessness and fear know the peace of God." (*The Patrician.*)

Although the austerity of the Sussex Downs, their Englishness and reticence, occupied a special place in Galsworthy's affection, his allegiance was not undivided. So much beauty, and so varied, is crowded between the coasts of England that one who loved her might spend all his days passing from one scene of delight to another. Galsworthy travelled the world more than most men; delighted in contact with foreign places and yielded to their fascination; but it was the beauty of England, and particularly of Sussex and Devon, that awakened his deepest emotion. Perhaps he felt for his native land what Felix, also a novelist and endowed with many of the qualities possessed by Galsworthy, felt: a kind of sensuous chivalry, a passion based on her charm, on her tranquillity, on the power she had to draw him into her embrace, to make him feel that he had come from her, from her alone, and into her alone was going back. There was ever to him a special flavour about the elm-girt fields, the flowery coppices, a special fascination in its full, white-clouded skies, its grass-edged roads, its pied and creamy cattle, and the blue-green loam of the Malvern Hills. Felix pondered on the Land—a marvellous sweet thing, when all was said. Changing its sheen and texture, the feel of its air, its very scent, from day to day. This land with its myriad offspring of flowers and flying folk; the majestic and untiring march of seasons: Spring and its wistful ecstasy of saplings, and its yearning, wild, wind-loosened heart; gleam and song, blossom and cloud, and the swift white rain; each up-turned leaf so little and so glad to flutter; each wood and field so full of peeping things! Summer! Ah! Summer, when on the solemn old trees the long days shone and lingered, and the glory of the meadows and the murmur of life and the scent of flowers bewildered the hours, till surcharge of warmth and beauty brooded into dark passion, and broke! And autumn, in mellow haze down on the fields and woods; smears of gold already on the beeches, smears of crimson on the rowans, the apple-trees still burdened, and a flax-blue sky well-nigh merging with the misty air; the cattle browsing in the lingering golden stillness; not a breath to fan the blue smoke of the weed-fires—and in the fields no one moving—who would disturb such mellow peace? And winter! The long spaces, the long dark; and yet—and yet, what delicate loveliness of twig tracery; what blur of rose and brown and purple caught in the bare boughs and in the early sunset sky! What sharp dark flights of birds in the grey-white firmament!

Not often does Galsworthy rhapsodise so consciously as this. It is as if the heroine of *The Freelands* were the earth itself, and claimed this tribute to her virtues and charms. The book is impregnated with an aching love of the country, whose beauty moves to unaccustomed eloquence so unpromisingly matter-of-fact a man as Stanley, the unimaginative. Travelling along grass-bordered roads, the beauty of England struck his not too-sensitive spirit and made him almost gasp. It was that moment of the year when the countryside seems to faint from its own loveliness, from the intoxication of its scents and sounds. Creamy-white hawthorns, splashed here and there with crimson, flooded the hedges in breaking waves of flower-foam; the fields were all buttercup glory; every tree had its cuckoo calling; every bush its blackbird or thrush in full evensong. Swallows were flying rather low, and the sky, whose moods they watch, had the slumberous, surcharged beauty of a long, fine day, with showers not far away. Some orchards were still in blossom, and the great wild bees, hunting over flowers and grasses warm to their touch, kept the air deeply murmurous. Movement, light, colour, song, scent, the warm air, and the fluttering leaves were confused, till one had almost become the other.

And Stanley thought, for he was not rhapsodic: "Wonderful pretty country! The way everything's looked after—you never see it abroad!"

How loath Galsworthy always was to leave the bees—usually wild bees—without their special word!

JOHN GALSWORTHY
The wild bees beat
Their drums and sack the blossom bowers.

They buzz in and out of his books as if he had a special affection for them—which indeed he had. I recall a hovering bee which circled round lovers' heads in *The Patrician*, scenting, it seemed, the honey in their hearts, and a dusky adventurer, attracted by the scent of lilies in Miltoun's library, who filled the room with his pleasant humming; busy bees on the snapdragons, and a humble-bee booming into the dining-room of the Reverend Edward Pierson.

Scarcely less inevitable, the blossoms of fruit-trees. Most memorable, perhaps that orchard in *The Apple-Tree* at night, conjured up with such wizardry that we share Ashurst's longing and apprehension. He moved a step or two, and again halted, aware of a dim living whiteness all round his head. On the dark unstirring trees, innumerable flowers and buds all soft and blurred, were being bewitched to life by the creeping moonlight. He had the oddest feeling of actual companionship, as if a million white moths or spirits had floated in and settled between dark sky and darker ground, and were opening and shutting their wings on a level with his eyes. And among these quivering, haunted, moon-witched trees he was seized with doubts of everything. All was unearthly here, fit for no earthly lovers; fit only for god and goddess, faun and nymph.

Galsworthy was very sensitive to the magic of the night, endowing it with many moods and fancies. That summer evening when Mark Lennan, ill with longing, waited for his beloved, lingers unforgettably in the memory. The moon would not rise till ten. And all things waited. The creatures of night were

slow to come forth after that long bright summer's
day, watching for the shades of the trees to sink
deeper and deeper into the now chalk-white water;
watching for the chalk-white face of the sky to be
masked with velvet. The very black-plumed trees
themselves seemed to wait in suspense for the grape-
bloom of night. All things stared, wan in that hour
of parting day—all things had eyes wistful and un-
blessed. In those moments glamour was so dead that
it was as if meaning had abandoned the earth. But
not for long. Winged with darkness, it stole back;
not the soul of meaning that had gone, but a witch-
like and brooding spirit harbouring in the black
trees, in the high dark spears of the rushes, and on the
grim-snouted snags that lurked along the river bank.
And in the wood there began a cruel bird tragedy—
some dark pursuit in the twilight above the bracken;
the piercing shrieks of a creature into whom talons
have again and again gone home; and mingled with
them, hoarse raging cries of triumph. Many minutes
they lasted, those noises of the night, sound-emblems
of all the cruelty in the heart of Nature; till at last
death appeased that savagery. And any soul abroad,
that pitied fugitives, might once more listen and not
weep. Then a nightingale began to give forth its
long liquid gurgling; and a corncrake churred in the
young wheat. Again the night brooded, in the silent
tops of the trees, in the more silent depths of the
water. It sent out at long intervals a sigh or murmur,
a tiny scuttling splash, an owl's hunting cry. And its
breath was still hot and charged with heavy odour,
for no dew was falling. (*The Dark Flower.*)

Another night imbued with the awareness of evil
is seen through the eyes of Barbara. (*The Patrician.*)
It was one of those nights, dark yet gleaming, when

there seems a flying malice in the heavens; when the stars, from under and above the black clouds, are like eyes frowning and flashing down at men with purposed malevolence. The great sighing trees, even, had caught this spirit, save one, a dark, spire-like cypress, planted three hundred and fifty years before, whose tall form incarnated the very spirit of tradition, and neither swayed nor soughed like the others. From her, too close-fibred, too resisting, to admit the breath of Nature, only a dry rustle came. Still almost exotic, in spite of centuries of sojourn, and now brought to life by the eyes of night, she seemed almost terrifying in her narrow, spear-like austerity, as though something had dried and died within her soul.

With Barbara, too, in a somewhat happier mood, we have a view of London seen by night from the roof of a tall mansion. High above all neighbouring houses, she was almost appalled by the majesty of what she saw. This night-clothed city, so remote and dark, so white-gleaming and alone, on whose purple hills and valleys grew such myriad golden flowers of light, from whose heart came this deep incessant murmur—could it possibly be the same city through which she had been walking that very day! From its sleeping body the supreme wistful spirit had emerged in dark loveliness, and was low flying down there tempting her. Barbara turned round, to take in all that amazing prospect, from the black glades of Hyde Park, in front, to the powdery white ghost of a church tower, away to the East. How marvellous was this city of night! And as, in presence of that wide darkness of the sea before dawn, her spirit had felt little and timid within her—so it felt now, in face of this great, brooding beautiful creature, whom man had made. She singled out the shapes and tower of Westminster and Whitehall; and everywhere the inextricable loveliness of dim blue forms and sinuous pallid lines of light, under an indigo-dark sky.

Galsworthy rarely if ever panders to his love of nature by calling up irrelevant facts or indulging his skill as a landscape artist; sometimes, notably, of course, in *The Freelands*, the country is used as a theme running contrapuntally, as it were, to the theme of the human characters, meeting it at appropriate points, and, like a good counter-theme, occasionally colliding with it and producing a significant discord. When nature's mood and man's mood are in concord, how sweet the resultant harmony! When they are in conflict, how poignant, how painful the discord! Dinny (*Flowering Wilderness*), bereaved of her lover, in despair over her father's poverty, escapes from the stress of watching human eyes. The last dregs of the long daylight had drained down beyond the rim, but warmth abode, for no air stirred, and no dew fell—a still, dry, dark night, with swarming stars. From the moment she stepped out Dinny was lost in it. But the old house shrouded in its creepers lived for her eyes, a dim presence with four still-lighted windows. She stood under an elm tree, leaning against its trunk, with her arms stretched back and her hands clasping it behind her. Night was a friend —no eye to see, no ear to listen. She stared into it, unmoving, drawing comfort from the solidity and breadth behind her. Moths flew by, almost touching her face. Insentient nature, warm, incurious, busy even in the darkness. Millions of little creatures burrowed and asleep, hundreds floating or creeping about, billions of blades of grass and flowers straightening up ever so slowly in the comparative coolness of the night. Nature! Pitiless and indifferent even to the only creatures who crowned and petted her with pretty words! Threads broke and hearts broke, or whatever really happened to the silly things— Nature twitched no lips, heaved no sigh! One twitch of Nature's lip would have been more to her than all human sympathy. If, as in the "Birth of Venus", breezes could puff at her, waves like doves lap at her feet, bees fly round her seeking honey! If for one moment in this darkness she could feel at one with the starshine, the smell of earth, the twitter of the bat, the touch of a moth's wing on her nose!

And how trees crowd the Galsworthy canvas, almost, one might say, people the Galsworthy world, for they live in independence, endowed with personality and indiosyncrasies. To him, as to Harold Monro, "a tree seems something more than tree," sentient and individual. The birch-tree, above all, held some special magic for him and often claimed his attention. Once he uses it "contrapuntally", in *The Country House*. The Squire's lady has gone, the gentle Margery Pendyce than whom none could have appeared less rebellious, and the Squire, admitting nothing, knew within him that with her gone his life's foundations were in danger of crumbling. He rode down the main aisle of the home covert. The June foliage made one long colonnade, broken by a winding river of sky. Among the oaks and hazels, the beeches and the elms, the ghostly body of a birch-tree shone here and there, captured by those grosser trees which seemed to cluster round her, proud of their prisoner, loath to let her go, that subtle spirit of their wood. They knew that, were she gone, their forest lady, wilder and yet gentler than themselves—

they would lose credit, lose the grace and essence of their corporate being.

The birch-trees in the place which was known as Fairyland (*Inn of Tranquillity*) are more beautiful than any in the world; and when the clouds are streaming over in rain-grey, and the sky soaring above in higher blue, just seen, those gold and silver creatures have such magical loveliness as makes the heart of mortals ache. And the lime trees, gold with flowers, whose perfume fills so many moments in the Galsworthy saga! Once, on a July afternoon, close to a large lime tree, the bees were busy among her long, drooping, honey-coloured blossoms; the wind was fluttering all her leaves, swaying her boughs, and drifting her scent towards the writer. She was in a tumult; the wind had entered her heart and her shivering gust of emotion was such that one could not choose but look at her. It was the passion one sees when bees are swarming—a fierce, humming swirl of movement, as though she had suddenly gone mad with life and love. But soon this tumult died away; she was once more a perfumed, gracious, delicately alluring tree. It was a passionate lime tree, too, it will be remembered, that taunted the unlovable, unloving Bianca as she walked in Hyde Park.

BIRDS, BEASTS AND FISHES

BIRDS, BEASTS AND FISHES

BIRDS, beasts, and—well, hardly fishes: fishes only make their appearance at the end of a line or on a dish—but birds and beasts, with insects innumerable, filled an important part of Galsworthy's world. In paddock, on the racecourse and in the hunting field, horses; in the hunting field, but particularly in the home, dogs; an occasional cat, and myriads of singing birds and humming insects. Worms are not neglected, nor even earwigs; and there is at least one lovely cow with lustrous eyes. No wonder, thought Young Jolyon, the legend put Christ in a manger. What more devotional than the eyes and moon-white horns of a chewing cow in the warm dusk?

Galsworthy took to animals that same desire to understand which distinguished his approach to humans. The so-called love of animals is frequently only the polite classification of a much less admirable emotion: the satisfaction of a wish to master something weaker than oneself. Domesticated dogs are by nature slaves, willing slaves rejoicing in their bonds, and they delight in pandering to their masters' or mistresses' desire for power. Being human, Galsworthy probably shared this almost universal attitude towards the animal kingdom, but in a much less degree than most men. He respected animals. He respected their individuality; he indulged their funny little ways; and he did not expect them to conform to his. Horses and dogs in particular peopled his life and his books; cats, although they had a place in both, were relegated to downstairs. That was the dogs' doing. The dogs had the freedom of the house, and the cats—secretive, independent creatures—scorning canine familiarity with another species, kept themselves to themselves. Cats, in Galsworthy's books, are just cats: dogs are individuals, with as definitely marked characteristics as the human characters with whom they share the honours. No Galsworthy cat, complete with shape and colour, remains in my memory. I remember that it was a cat of sorts that unloosed the emotion which till that moment Soames, faced with the returned but broken figure of Irene, had bottled up. As he walked in the square where his house was, a half-starved cat rubbed along the garden railings towards him. Presently something soft touched his legs, the cat was rubbing herself against them. And a sob that shook him from head to foot burst from Soames's chest.

It was another cat—just "cat", unnamed and undifferentiated—that showed dumb unwitting sympathy with another social misfit, the Reverend Edward Pierson, slithering under the wicket gate, arching her back and rubbing herself against his leg, crinkling and waving the tip of her tail. Pierson bent down and stroked the creature's head; but, uttering a faint miaou, the cat stepped daintily across the road. The observation here is as exact as Galsworthy's always was, but the cat is no more marked out from other cats than that dripping creature which the parson in *The Island Pharisees* brought in out of the rain, comforting it with a "poor pussy, poor pussy!" condescendingly, his voice like nothing human in its cracked superiority. Even the little Persian kitten in

Fraternity is a type rather than an individual. She seemed to say, as she gazed into her mistress's face: "I am of a piece with you and everything around you. We are both elegant and rather slender; we both love warmth and kittens . . ."

But the dogs! How many, varied, clearly-defined, they are! Not by any means always admirable, or even likeable, they nevertheless command one's respect because they do not pretend to be what they are not. Any tendency to sentimentalise dogs which Galsworthy may have had—and I think it is there— is mitigated by his capacity to keep his eyes open to their failings. One of the most interesting of his lady dogs was Miranda, the little moonlight-coloured bulldog bitch, of toy breed, with eyes like agates, who had been handed down clearer and paler with each generation, till she had at last lost all the peculiar virtues of dogs that bait the bull. Miranda was a perfect lady, whose virtue, it will be remembered, was one day rewarded by the finding of the perfect gentleman, stuffed and sterilised, price 4s. 6d. She was blessed, too, with the perfect master, Hilary, who she knew would never hold her mouth ajar and watch her teeth, as some men do; that when she was lying on her back, he would gently rub her chest without giving her the feeling that she was doing wrong, as women will; and if she sat with her eyes fixed on his study fire, he would never prevent her thinking of the nothing she loved to think on. Even Miranda, it will be seen, was not allowed to exist without throwing some light on one of the principal characters in *Fraternity*. Her qualities were the negative ones of sinlessness, but she was not entirely without charm, and certainly appreciated her master, going so far in unrestraint on one occasion as to spring on to his unresisting lap, placing her arms on his chest and licking his face all over.

I feel that if questions of breeding might be disregarded, Miranda's perfect mate would have been John the Spaniel in *The Country House*, that model of servility which clung to its master's feet with so much persistency that he was inevitably kicked a good many times during the course of every day. Miranda might have trained him to attain to the perfection of her stuffed and sterilised toy dog, "plus a little something" as the advertisements say. But they did not meet. He was before her time. Perfect picture of servility though he was, John had not an infallible sense of the right thing to do in order to ingratiate himself in his master's favour. His knowledge of human psychology had lacunæ which allowed him to misjudge his master's mood on that day when the Squire was sick and sore because his wife had run away from him. John took two and a half brace of his master's slippers, and placing them in unaccustomed spots, lay on them one by one till they were warm, and then left them for some bird or other to hatch out. But the scolding he received for this ill-advised behaviour made him love his master the more, so deep was his devotion; and when the deserted Squire slowly mounted the stairs to seek a lonely bed, it was the spaniel John who, like a shadow, mounted behind him.

Blink, Mr. Lavender's faithful hound, was compounded of that blend of sagacity and stupidity characteristic of sheep dogs and had other traits that distinguished her. When Mr. Lavender, aspiring to war oratory, half-deliriously cried aloud that we should never sheath the sword until the cause of humanity and chivalry was safe once more, Blink,

ever uneasy about sounds which seemed to her to have no meaning, stood on her hind legs and endeavoured to stay them by licking his face. The complacent stupidity of Blink treading under into the pond the hat which she had been encouraged to salve, is graphically described. (*The Burning Spear*.)

Very definite, too, is the personality of Ting-a-ling, Fleur's Pekinese: proud, self-centred, and a snob, but paradoxically enough, likeable in spite of his failings. Ting-a-ling was not his baptismal name. When *The White Monkey* was published serially he was known as Confucius, but Galsworthy received a letter from the Reverend John Hedley in which the following passage occurred:

> "I think I know the Chinese people fairly well, and I am sure that they will resent the use of that name for a dog. Don't think me extravagant if I say that I would as soon think of naming a dog after the Man of Nazareth as after the Sage of China,"

upon receiving which Galsworthy took steps to change the dog's name. He had called him Confucius because *The White Monkey* was intended to give a picture of modern youth in all its irreverence, but he had overlooked the possibility of giving offence to the Chinese, for whom he had a great admiration. And that is how Confucius became Ting-a-ling. The pampered little creature was shrewd enough to get round even Soames, who indulged him on one occasion with salted almonds. "Believe the little brute likes me," thought Soames; "he's always looking at me." He touched the dog's nose with the tip of his finger and Ting-a-ling gave it a slight lick with his curly blackish tongue. Cupboard love, probably, but it gave Soames the sensation which of all others he most lacked—that of being liked for his own sake.

Foch, the dog which Dinny and Wilfrid rescued from the Home for Lost Dogs, bore an unblemished character, as devoted as only a spaniel can be, and less servile than some are. But the most complete portrait of a dog is to be found, of course, in "Memories," the last prose piece in *The Inn of Tranquillity*. From the moment when the puppy is met at Waterloo Station, nose swollen from crying and from being pressed against things that he could not see through; hammerheaded, with no eyes at all, and little connection between his head, his body and his legs, ears very long, and a disgraceful white patch to mar his blackness, he goes straight to his mistress's heart and ours. His story provides Galsworthy with many openings for generalisation about men and beasts, and I suppose it was here that he made the first explicit confession of his over-mastering aversion from killing those birds and creatures of which his pet was so fond as soon as they were dead; an attitude which was revealed implicitly, however, in much earlier work, notably in *The Country House*. His descriptions of shooting have that atmosphere of excitement which could only have been given to them by one who had at some time or other enjoyed it; and thus, by allowing us to share vicariously in the pleasure of the sport, he gives us the greater shock when with equal vividness he describes the suffering which crowns it. When George Pendyce brings down a pheasant, and a smirk of triumph plays on his lips because he was feeling the joy of life, we momentarily share his sensations; but before many seconds have elapsed our author is tabulating the many ways in which suffering may be inflicted on the creatures, and winds up his chapter with a picture of a wounded rabbit lying on its side, its fore-legs raised like the hands of a praying child. Motion-less as death, all its remaining life was centred in its black soft eyes. Uncomplaining, ungrudging, un-knowing, with that poor soft wandering eye, it was going back to Mother Earth.

His love for horses seems to have had very few reservations. Even when, as in *Beyond*, a horse is the instrument of a tragic disaster, blame is withheld from the animal and fastened on the master. If Sum-merhay had not had a habit of thrusting and too light hands, or if his own inward turmoil had not communicated itself to the animal Hotspur, the six-teen-hand brown horse, would not have got out of control and run his master to sudden death. A horse's faults are bound up with the refusal to be broken in to the will of somebody who has no divine right of mastery and are therefore less reprehensible than admirable. To this particular kind of breaking-in Galsworthy had no deep objection, believing probably that the horse was compensated by pleasurable excitement and good living for what it lost in freedom; but for horse-racing, admitting its attractions, his approval was qualified, as is shown by his description of Newmarket Heath as the place where, by a judicious admixture of whip and spur, oats and whisky, horses are caused to place one leg before another with unnecessary rapidity, in order that men may exchange little pieces of metal with the greater freedom. (*The Country House.*)

Without adopting the technique of the catalogue, however, it would be impossible to refer specifically to the almost countless felicities to be found among Galsworthy's references to animals. His eye for their beauty and attributes, their peculiarities and charms, was unfailingly just. The time, place and manner of a bird's song are always accurately introduced, for their own sake and also for their place in the psychological scheme of the story; dogs' tails are seen moving "humbly;" we are made aware of the "old-maidish way" of partridges; we see the "little inquiring head" of a tortoise, and meet a flock of goats, "solemnly curious, with their queer yellow oblong-pupilled eyes;" and owls, always sure of a friendly word from Galsworthy, have a paragraph to themselves in *The Patrician*. No owl was ever shot on the Monkland Court estate, and these soft-flying spirits of the dusk hooted and hunted, to the great benefit of all except the creeping voles. One May, when the weather was really warm, so that joy of life was in the voles, they found those succulent creatures of an extraordinarily pleasant flavour, and on them each pair was bringing up a family of exceptionally fine little owls, very solemn, with big heads, bright large eyes, and wings as yet only able to fly downwards.

For thoughtlessly tethered animals, for captive birds, for "tamed and shabby tigers"—to quote a poet, Ralph Hodgson, for whom Galsworthy had a great liking—, for pursued things and caged things of all kinds, pit ponies, lost and abandoned dogs, Galsworthy had an unending compassion which was in line with the rest of his outlook on a predatory world.

"PITY IS TRIPE"

"PITY IS TRIPE"

It has indeed been charged against him with some persistence that his habit of pity was weak and mechanical, born of a conventional if sincere humanitarianism. There is a character in *Joy*, Miss Beach, whose over-tender heart has been cited as almost a replica of Galsworthy's own. The words "Poor creature!" express her customary attitude. A pot of worms prepared as bait for fishing excites her to exclaim: "Don't hurt the poor creatures!" She swallows a fly and her first concern is for the "poor creature" thus deprived of life. "I hate suffering," she says on another occasion; "if it's only a fly, I hate it." And hearing that ten earwigs have been killed in the spare bedroom, all she can say is "Poor creatures!" To identify Galsworthy with this superabundant and misplaced pity seems to me inept. The very fact that he makes the expression of excessive pity the occasion for laughter ought to be evidence enough of his awareness of the danger of overcompassion.

Nevertheless, it cannot be denied that he had his share of that ingrained over-tenderness of soul under which Shelton in *The Island Pharisees* groaned and that the sight or thought of suffering moved him more profoundly than they move the average sensual man. Being by nature both artist and reformer, it was inevitable that the driving force of compassion should influence his choice of subject and in part govern his treatment of it. There cannot be too much joy and happiness in the world, nor too much beauty, and if cruelty and callousness, thoughtlessness and lack of sympathy, shown the image of themselves in play and novel, are so horrified by the sight that they run away and hide, the reformer who craves for beauty, joy and happiness, will not hesitate to employ the artist who can work the miracle. Galsworthy the reformer, beholding the iniquities perpetrated in the name of Justice, Nationalism, Society, Religion, Property, and the other gods, called up Galsworthy the artist and bade him expose the iniquities, and he obeyed. Upholders of the doctrine of Art for Art's sake will be quick to say "Then he was no artist;" but unless we are willing to scrap every considerable dramatist who ever existed, from Shakespeare to Shaw, with a backward glance to include Sophocles, Euripides and the other Greeks, we shall have to admit that propaganda and literary and dramatic art, so far from being incompatible, are almost inseparable companions.

If Galsworthy's pity had been called forth by objects unworthy of it, it would be indefensible; if it had been directed toward those who had no need of it or were weakened by it, it would be redundant and pernicious. Did it ever take these forms? In general, no; in one matter, yes. Where he seems to me to have gone astray is in his treatment of the poor. To him to be poor was almost synonymous with being pitiable. It is not easy to recall a really happy poor person in the whole of Galsworthy's work. The poor in his plays are almost invariably oppressed, lacking in vitality, pitiable. Given the circumstances in which he places them, the pity is justified, but a more

balanced picture would have introduced characters
equally poor but at least as happy in their struttings
on the surface of an imperfect earth as the rich or
well-to-do. Mrs. Jones one accepts because Mrs.
Jone's lugubricity does not diminish her vitality, but
Mrs. Jones is no more typical of the genus charwoman than Dean Inge is typical of the *genus ecclesias-
ticus*. The young man Bicket in *The White Monkey*
and his pretty little wife Victorine may be accepted,
also, for their inherent vitality, and the pathos with
which Galsworthy invests their lot is legitimate; but
when Michael Mont, having befriended the young
fellow in spite of his lapse—it will be remembered
that he stole books from his employers—and sees
that his eyes are swimming, we are constrained to
share his fear that he is being sentimental and to
recall the maxim which haunts him—"Pity is tripe—
pity is tripe."

It is a soldier, Fort in *Saint's Progress*, who puts the
matter in a nutshell. "These are times of action," he
says. "Philosophy seems to mean nothing nowadays.
The one thing is to hate tyranny and cruelty, and
protect everything that's weak and lonely. It's all
that's left to make life worth living, when all the
packs of all the world are out for blood." Nobody
with the average amount of altruistic feeling could
find much to object to in this code of conduct and
Galsworthy does not depart from it. All that could
be urged against him in this connection is that in
finding so many objects of pity he is giving a lopsided
view of life. But except in his treatment of the human
poor, I do not think that he could be proved guilty.

It is true that he was not given to the creation of
heroic figures, larger than life; but he called up many
fine men and women towards whom, even in their

defeat, pity is not the emotion aroused, and too much stress has been laid on the fact that one of his chief characters, Falder in *Justice*, was so weak that he was doomed to be crushed by the gods sooner or later, whether on the wheel of the Law or more meanly. Because *Justice* is one of his best-known plays, it is too often taken as typical. But there are many cases where characters stand up to the blind or malignant attacks of impersonal forces, and, though defeated, remain unbroken. Stephen More in *The Mob*, Michael Strangway in *A Bit o' Love*, the antagonists Roberts and Anthony in *Strife*, and many others in the plays alone, while the novels teem with characters, men and women, who stand up to fate with courage, and when they go down, go down with dignity. There are instances in which the legitimate emotion evoked is compassion. Poor Ferse (*Maid in Waiting*), for example, mentally-deranged, who finds death preferable to life lived in a torment of doubt, is one such example. Adrian, finding his body, knew that he ought to be thankful for the sake of the dead man as well as for his wife, but he could feel nothing but that profound pity for a fellow man so tortured and broken in his prime— profound pity, and a sort of creeping identification with the mystery of Nature enwrapping the dead man and his resting-place.

Galsworthy confessed in the Preface to *The Man of Property* that he pitied Soames, the tragedy of whose life was the uncontrollable tragedy of being unlovable; and this pity is not shown by making Soames weak, timid, unattractive, but by faithfully recording such characteristics as should, if there were justice in life, permit of his being loved, and yet fail to do so. When he knew that his wife's lover was with her, he dawdled about in his dressing-room, and when he went downstairs, purposely shut the door loudly to warn them that he was coming. When his father protested that Irene had had too much liberty, Soames says: "I won't have anything said against her." He did his best, but it was no good: he was unwanted and lonely. One is glad that as old age approached, a certain mellowness came upon him and he found affection in his realist daughter, Fleur; but even so, the full force of her love never found expression until he was on his death-bed.

That Galsworthy was aware of the danger of excessive compassion is evident from the beginning. The almost unavoidable corollary of a hatred of cruelty and injustice is an immoderate capacity for sympathising with the victims, and Galsworthy, having the former in an inordinate degree, was in danger of the latter also. Even the inflicters of cruelty, being themselves the victims of an inescapable environment, were a subject for pity rather than for blame. An extreme example of this is, of course, derived from war, in which victim and villain are so inextricably confused that only omniscience could rightly apportion blame. The crowd cheered when a Zeppelin burst into flames. The Reverend Edward Pierson's first thought was "The poor men in it! How terrible!" but his daughter Noel, hard and pitiless, retorted: "They needn't have come. They're murderers." And the bewildered clergyman prays: "O God, Who in Thy great mercy hath delivered us from peril, take into Thy keeping the souls of these our enemies, consumed by Thy wrath before our eyes; give us the power to pity them—men like ourselves." Backwards and forwards his thoughts go—now pitying the victims, now triumphant in their defeat.

RELIGION AND MORTALITY

RELIGION AND MORTALITY

"THE ETERNAL MOOD AT WORK" . . .

On no subject was Galsworthy so tentative as on the subject of religion. A mind like his, essentially logical and well-controlled, could not become the servant of a dogmatic creed; and one whose chief function as a writer was to analyse and question the accepted bases of human society would be unlikely to bend the knee before an authoritarian conception of the universe. This is not to say that he was unmoved by the wonder and mystery of life, but rather to emphasise the fact that his interest and deep concern were more especially concentrated on the world of men where human plants thrive and die, human weeds flourish and fade under the fresh, impartial skies (*Island Pharisees*) rather than upon a mystical religion which attempted to explain and justify such disparities.

It will be found that in the Galsworthy world, which is abundantly peopled with officials, there are relatively few clergymen, and on the whole they do not make a very brave show. One remembers the Reverend Hussell Barter, drawn with a fidelity and understanding that do little to make him more attractive. With every desire to do him justice Galsworthy seems unable to withhold little touches which excite the reader's scorn within a few minutes of having aroused friendlier feelings. The "little rueful boy" who waits downstairs while his long-suffering wife groans in labour, adding to an already too-plentiful family, awakens our pity. The words he had spoken so many times left him as though of malice. "We are all in the hands of God." And then, when the child is born, he hurries to his study, locks the door, kneels down, and remains there many minutes, thinking of nothing, adds our author, with that tiny touch of malice which probably reveals a fundamental dislike of the type he has been describing, not altogether unsympathetically.

There is also the clergyman Michael Strangway in *A Bit o' Love*, an idealist of the purest water, to whom reference has been made in another chapter (*page* 43) and the Parson in *Escape*, who gives sanctuary to the escaped convict—also a sympathetic figure; but the most lovable of all Galsworthy's clergymen is Uncle Hilary, who first appears in *Maid in Waiting* and afterwards in *Flowering Wilderness* and *Over the River*. But what sort of a clergyman is this, whose views are so broad that if they were known he would be unfrocked? Clearly it is not to his clergymen that we must turn for an expression of Galsworthy's own religious outlook, but to the utterances scattered about his work and bearing internal or external evidence of their identity with his own views.

As a young man, and in his early middle years, he was so absorbed in the phenomena of social life, so alive to social injustices, that religion occupied a subordinate place in his mind. As he grew older his thoughts dwelt more frequently on transcendental matters and he seems drawn towards a half-mystical philosophy. In his later work, however, a note of greater scepticism can be heard and he puts into the mouths of some of his characters a bitterness, verging on cynicism, from which his earlier work is free.

RELIGION AND MORTALITY

Religion plays little or no part in the scheme of *The Man of Property*; in so far as it does, it is shown as a tacit acceptance of mechanical forces beyond the ken of man. Young Jolyon, who had the impersonal eye, looks upon his father, Old Jolyon, the figurehead of his family and class and creed, the representative of moderation, and order, and love of property, in the gloomy comfort of his room, a puppet in the power of great forces that cared nothing for family or class or creed, but moved, machine-like, with dread processes to inscrutable ends.

Nature, poetically personified, is endowed with a quaint irony which works revolutions in men's hearts, and even Soames, of all Galsworthy's characters probably the least susceptible to the call of Nature, is not unmoved by the voice of spring which breathes into a man an ineffable yearning, a painful sweetness, a longing that makes him stand motionless, looking at the leaves of grass, and fling out his arms to embrace he knows not what. The conviction that the forces of the universe are beyond our knowing seems to persist throughout the earlier works. It is mockery to talk of justice. There is no justice for men, for they are ever in the dark. Small, of no import; insects to be crushed and made an end of when the machine comes full circle. The blackness of this pessimism, not laboured but implicit, is not dispelled by *Fraternity*, the book which followed *The Man of Property*. Determinism still colours the author's thought. We are like flies caught among the impalpable and smoky threads of cobwebs; so men struggle in the webs of their own natures, giving here a start, there a pitiful small jerking, long sustained, and failing into stillness. Enmeshed they were born, enmeshed they die, fighting according to their strength to the end; to fight, in the hope of freedom, their joy; to die, not knowing they are beaten, their reward. But somewhat inconsistently, it appears to be assumed that there is some power outside man's nature, which is named Life with a capital initial letter, that devises for each man the particular dilemmas most suited to his nature.

This consciousness of pitiless forces governing the destiny of man, whether blindly or deliberately, becomes less insistent in later works, some of which exhale a mild pagan mysticism. It would not be too much to identify Galsworthy with the spirit of exaltation which raised Miltoun (*The Patrician*) out of the imprisoning flesh. Reaching the top of a tor in Devon he beheld land and sky transcending even his exaltation. It was like a symphony of great music; or the nobility of a stupendous mind laid bare; it was God up there, in His many moods. Serenity was spread in the middle heavens, blue, illimitable; and along to the East, three huge clouds, like thoughts brooding over the destinies below, moved slowly towards the sea, so that great shadows filled the valleys. And the land that lay under all the other sky was gleaming and quivering with every colour, as it were, clothed with the divine smile. There was no sound, no scent, and it seemed to Miltoun as if his spirit had left his body, and become part of the solemnity of God.

In *The Inn of Tranquillity*, written round about this time, much the same feelings and thoughts find a place, expressed more directly from Galsworthy's own standpoint. The Italian hotel proprietor, newly returned from America—that grotesque little vulgarian in the skittle-alley, wearing a bowler hat, a bright brown suit, pink tie, and very yellow boots, who when complimented on the position of his hotel which, under a burning blue sky, commanded a view of the Odyssean coast, rich in pine-trees and junipers, cypresses and olives, replied in admirable English "Too bloody quiet," provokes the author to meditate in this fashion: Suddenly I was visited by a sensation only to be described as a sort of smiling certainty, emanating from, and, as it were, still tingling within every nerve of myself, but yet vibrating harmoniously with the world around. It was as if I had suddenly seen what was the truth of things, not perhaps to anybody else, but at all events to me. And I felt at once tranquil and elated, as when something is met with which rouses and fascinates in a man all his faculties. 'For,' I thought, 'if it is ridiculous in me to despise my friend—that perfect marvel of disharmony —it is ridiculous in me to despise anything. If *he* is a little bit of continuity, as perfectly logical an expression of a necessary phrase or mood of existence as I myself am, then, surely, there is nothing in all the world that is not a little bit of continuity, the expression of a little necessary mood. 'Yes,' I thought, 'he and I, and those olive-trees, and this spider on my hand, and everything in the Universe which has an individual shape, are all fit expressions of the separate moods of a great underlying Mood or Principle, which must be perfectly adjusted, volving and revolving on itself. For if It did not volve and revolve on itself, It would peter out at one end or the other, and the image of this petering out no man with his mental apparatus can conceive.'

And so he goes on, developing his thought, in a way which would probably find acceptance among those Indian philosophers who preach the Karmic law of cause and effect, and concludes that a man may not despise any one or any thing, not even a skittle alley, for they are threaded to him and to despise them would be to blaspheme against continuity, and to blaspheme against continuity would be to deny Eternity. One cannot help loving. One cannot help hating. But contempt is the sovereign idiocy.

It would be unfair to attribute to Galsworthy all the religious views expressed in *The Patrician*, but in line with the above personal avowal is the assertion of Courtier: "When I get up and when I go to bed, when I draw a breath, see a face, or a flower, or a tree—if I didn't feel that I was looking on Deity, I believe I should quit this palace of varieties, from sheer boredom." And there is personal conviction in the reference to the old pagan rapture—an inexhaustible delight, a passionate soft acceptance of eternal fate, a wonderful acquiescence in the untiring mystery of life.

This surrendering to the universal was a recurring rather than a constant characteristic of Galsworthy. Too Western to have perpetual being in an atmosphere of mysticism, it was the occasion which prompted the state of mind and sent his thoughts beyond their accustomed range and his pen in pursuit of them, and the artist who recreated the mood which enabled us to share it. In one of his shorter pieces (*Buttercup Night*), so exactly does he reveal his intimacy with nature, that one has the sensation of having spent the night with him, sharing his experience and feeling life to be not merely a long picture-show for human eyes, but a single breathing, glowing, growing thing, of which we are no more important a part than the swallows and magpies, the foals and sheep in the meadows, the sycamores and ash trees and flowers in the fields, the rocks, and little bright streams, or even than the long fleecy clouds and their soft-shouting drivers, the winds. We remain with him through the silence of the night, with millions of living things snugly asleep all round. Insects, and flowers, birds, men, beasts, the very leaves on the trees; and waiting in imagination for the first bird to chirrup, we share his sense of the unity and communion of all life, of the subtle brotherhood of living things that fall all together into oblivion, and, all together, wake.

Remember, too, how Mark, the boy in *The Dark Flower*, disturbed by a love which somehow fails to satisfy, goes down to the river one morning unobserved and finds comfort in the crisp, gentle sound of water, and sits on a stone, very still, waiting for things to happen. You lost yourself that way, just became branches, and stones, and water, and birds, and sky. You did not feel such a beast . . . and years later, we find Mark, a middle-aged man, once more in the toils of passion, pacing the streets of London hour after hour, keeping always in the dark; not a star in the sky, not a human being spoken to or even clearly seen, not a bird or beast. . . A walk as lonely as the voyage of the human soul is lonely from birth to death with nothing to guide it but the flickering glow from its own frail spirit lighted it knows not where.

Here the Determinism is softened by the growing pagan mysticism, and in subsequent books it is even less prone to raise its head. Its place is usurped by an attitude which recalls Matthew Arnold's belief in that something not ourselves which makes for righteousness. "Do you believe in God?" asks Nedda in *The Freelands*, and Mr. Cuthbert, fencing a little and making play with the idea that God was nowadays It, Him or Her according to the believer's nature, confesses that although he would make no attempt to define what he meant by God, he nevertheless believes that there is in one some kind of instinct towards perfection that one will still feel when the lights are going out; some kind of honour forbidding one to let go and give up.

A state of mind, a finger-post erected by oneself to point the way, something subjective and personal: nothing outside oneself to which one could appeal, no tables of the Lord with commandments laid down inexorably and irrevocably, no Judge save one's own conscience—that, I suppose, would be Galsworthy's attitude at this time. It was no use to pray to the great mysterious Force which made one thing a cabbage, and the other a king; for That could obviously not be weak-minded enough to attend. One's mind is carried back to the child in *Villa Rubein*, Galsworthy's earliest novel, who felt that it was not brave to hope, because hope was prayer, and prayer was asking, and asking was not brave; and on to the most quoted of all Galsworthy's poems: "Make firm in me a heart too brave To ask Thee anything."

Beyond (1917) passes religion by, but *Saint's Progress*, two years later, although it adds little to our knowledge of Galsworthy's personal beliefs, is paradoxically enough primarily concerned with the progress of a clergyman, orthodox by conviction, in conflict with the forces of modernism, and with the erratic behaviour of men and women in a world made mad by war. Apart from the laying of the plot, a pivotal point of which is the birth of an illegitimate child to the saint's beloved daughter Noel, in this revealing that element of malice with which Galsworthy's attitude to the Church is so apt to be tinged—nothing could be more understanding than the author's treatment of this tragic figure of a man whose sensibilities and natural inclinations are in advance of his inherited and absorbed views. In none of Galsworthy's books is the name of God so frequently invoked, and in none with less sympathy. "I would rather think there's no God than a helpless or a wicked God," declared the girl Noel to her outraged father. Again: "Sometimes I hate the Church; either it's hard and narrow, or else it's worldly," and on the face of the poor saint comes a most strange look of pain and horror, as if an unspoken treachery of his own had been dragged forth for his inspection. The beginnings of scepticism are creeping into a mind which is not ripe to receive them. It is the tragedy of a man out of tune with his times. Galsworthy pities him, understands and even admires him, but he uses him as a scourge to attack an institution which he feels has outlived its function.

The Reverend Edward Pierson is the only full-length portrait of a clergyman. Drawn with compassionate understanding, the man is projected on to a screen peopled with characters who are so integral a part of the modern world that his isolation appears the more tragic. Nevertheless, with our pity for him there is an unavoidable admixture of impatience: we feel that a man of his intelligence and sensibility has no right to be the servant of outworn religious formulae; and this, plainly, is what Galsworthy intended our reaction should be. It is not without intention, either, that the Dean in *The Mob* is on the side of the worldly and against the idealist Stephen More.

JOHN GALSWORTHY

The Man of Property appeared in 1904; it was not until 1920 that *In Chancery* was issued, the fruits of the two preceding years. In the intervening space not only the Forsytes but Galsworthy had grown, and his treatment of them inevitably reflects, in part, the trend of his own mind. The old Forsytes had accepted the Church as an institution without believing in it as a religion; the younger generation, rejecting the Church, gropes towards belief. Old Jolyon, with his faith in property, upright conduct and, at the last, beauty, has passed away; Young Jolyon, who it will be remembered had the impersonal eye, is already leaving middle age behind, and the third of the series, Jolly, comes with the questioning mind of the late nineteenth century youth and demands a statement of faith from his father, who offers him two irreconcilable ideas of God—the Unknowable Creative Principle and the Sum of Altruism in man, in both of which one believes; and Christ is postulated as the link uniting the two conceptions and reconciling the apparently irreconcilable. Scepticism, practically amounting to disbelief, on the question of the survival of the human spirit after death, yields to a wistful hope, when the imminence of death sets his thoughts running on the subject, that he might see again those he loved.

It is not perhaps surprising that in neither the *Forsyte Saga* nor in *A Modern Comedy* does the author venture into other than terrestrial realms. A possessive world, the inhabitants of which cling fanatically to property palpable to the touch and visible to the bodily eye, has no ear for the choir invisible and no time for speculation apart from that which is reckoned in percentages. The generation to which *A Modern Comedy* is consecrated is largely composed of those disillusioned young people who grew up during the Great War and the hysterical ten years which followed it, when all values were in the melting-pot and everybody in thrall to the law which bade us take nothing seriously. In keeping religion almost entirely out of this half-dozen novels, Galsworthy, either instinctively, or, what is more probable, deliberately, demonstrated how non-religious, fundamentally, the Victorian era was and how sedulously the post-war generation shunned, as from fear, matters which affected its spiritual development.

As if the dam had been removed, the next batch of books teems with religious speculation, revealing, as I have said, a growing scepticism and an occasional bitterness. A world broken by war, plagued by the predatory instincts of the classes into whose hands the power seems to have fallen, an almost universal cynicism, may have played a part in disillusioning even so incorrigible an idealist as John Galsworthy. The questioning mind is certainly never far absent from his later books, and Dinny, the most fragrant and individual of all his young women, is a tormented creature whose only salvation is an abundant sense of humour. Her tentative belief in God, without knowing anything about it, as she confesses, becomes even more tentative as disaster follows disaster—not disasters in which she is personally involved but disasters which make her appalled by the chilly indifference of whatever gods may be before the spectacle of apparently meaningless suffering. Infinite invention going on in infinite stillness, which her sailor admirer had offered her as a definition of God, left her unconvinced. Such a God would not be of much immediate use to mortals. Would such a God hear and quiver when a hare was tortured by imperfect killing and cried in anguish? Would He make a note on His shirtcuff when stars hung cold and lightless a billion years hence? she broods sceptically. The million million leaves and blades of grass down there made the texture of the deeper darkness, the million million stars that gave the light by which she saw that darkness, all—all the result of perpetual motion in endless quiet, all part of God. And she herself, and the smoke of her cigarette, the jasmine under her nose, whose colour was invisible, and the movement of her brain, deciding that it was not yellow; that dog barking so far away that the sound was as a thread by which the woof of silence could be grasped; all—all endowed with the purpose remote, endless, pervading, incomprehensible of God. Existence seemed like a Shadow Show to her rather than Reality, and religion so dubious as to be useless. Belief in goodness for the sake of goodness, because goodness was beautiful, like a perfect flower, a starry night, a lovely tune—these were realities; but accept the mysterious ways of Providence? Who could? Insensate and cruel! One should behave decently because decency's the decent thing and not in hope of a reward.

"But why is decency the decent thing, Dinny, if there's no God?" asks her mother.

"O subtle and dear mother, I didn't say there wasn't God. I only said His Plan was too remote. Can't you hear God saying: 'By the way, is that ball the Earth still rolling?' And an Angel answering: 'Oh! Yes, Sir, quite nicely.' 'Let's see, it must be fungused over by now. Wasn't there some busy little parasite . . . ?' 'Oh! Yes, Sir, you mean man!' 'Quite, I remember we called it that.' "

Here we have the not very subtle outburst of an

unhappy girl, stung to facetious resentment by the inexorability of Nature; but it differs little in essence from the more carefully weighed and expressed opinions of Adrian, whose wisdom and knowledge are a byword. He would not say, as Dinny was provoked to say, that Providence was a "wash-out," because he did not belong to the generation which finds blasphemy piquant, but he, too disavows any belief in divine mercy in any form which we humans can understand, or in any way that we would exercise it ourselves. An all-embracing creativity and power of design without beginning and without end—obviously. But "tie it to our apron strings we can't," and his working version of God—the helping of man by man—is a harking-back to Young Jolyon's belief in God as the Sum of Altruism in Man.

As I write, Galsworthy's last novel—*Over the River* —comes into my hands, exhaling—or is it my fancy? —a faint aroma of disillusionment and mellow scepticism, the very title carrying a valedictory flavour. Dinny gazes at the unfeverish night. England silvered and indifferent to her fate, disbelieving in the Voice o'er Eden; old and permanent and beautiful even though the pound had gone off gold. . . . Men and their policies—how little they mattered, how soon they passed, a dissolving dew on the crystal immensity of God's toy! How queer—the passionate intensity of one's heart, and the incalculable cold callousness of Time and Space! To join, to reconcile? . . .

The rest, with John Galsworthy, is silence.

JOHN GALSWORTHY
"THE GRAVEN BEAUTY OF DEATH" . . .

The only certainty is death. Art and beauty, God and truth, love and the nature of goodness—these are subjective phenomena about which men may debate and wrangle, agree and fraternise, till the end of time; but about Death there is no disputing. It is the one certainty.

> "Behind the fairest masks of life
> Dwells ever that pale constant death . . ."

The way a man looks at death is therefore of unique interest, revealing his reaction to the one certainty. Death, like a purple thread, winds in and out of the texture of Galsworthy's work, pointing the passage of time, linking the generations. Sometimes it comes like a thief in the night and provides an unexpected climax; sometimes it is the violent but inevitable climax of a series of events; but generally it comes stealthily as Death comes in real life, gradually asserting its inexorability and claiming its always loath victim. By the way men die, you may know something of the way they have lived; by the way men behave in the presence of death, you may learn something about the contents of their minds and the quality of their personality. An author, therefore, whose work covers a long period does well not to pass too lightly over the way in which his characters quit the world.

The first important death in the Galsworthy cosmogony is that of Aunt Ann Forsyte. The manner of her dying is not described. The doctor, after one look at the old face, announced that she had passed away in her sleep. It was, perhaps, characteristic of Ann that she should pass away in her sleep: it seemed the kindest way of dying, giving least trouble.

RELIGION AND MORTALITY

One's thoughts are taken back to the opening chapter of *The Man of Property*—that priming of the Forsyte canvas preparatory to lining in the innumerable procession of Forsytes that was to fill it: Aunt Ann saying good-bye to the newly-engaged June, her fingertips pressing and pressing against each other, busy again with the recharging of her will against that inevitable ultimate departure of her own. Thus, although the death of Aunt Ann does not take place for another hundred pages, the core of mortality, the knowledge that death meant the relinquishing of property, is found to obsess the oldest of the Forsytes within a few pages of the opening of the *Saga*. Aunt Ann's whole existence was concentrated in the Family; it was her world and nothing else mattered. This it was that she would have to lay down when it came to her turn to die; this which gave to her that importance, that secret self-importance, without which none of us can bear to live; and to this she clung wistfully, with a greed that grew each day.

The passing of Ann gives Galsworthy an opportunity to enlighten us about those she left behind. Aunts Juley and Hester, overwhelmed, secretly felt it unreasonable of Ann to have left them without even a struggle; it was unlike a Forsyte to let go her grasp on life. Warm-hearted Juley could not bear the thought that Ann was lying there so cold. Aunt Hester, the silent, the patient, that back-water of the family energy, had also wept; but her guiding principle being the conservation of energy, she hoped the family would not want to rouse her into doing something. Doing something would not bring back Ann! James, resentful at not having been told sooner, declares that he knew how it would be. "I told you she wouldn't last through the summer."

And Aunt Hester refrains from telling him that it is nearly October.

The beautifying effect of death is constantly emphasised by Galsworthy. The figure of Aunt Ann in death is described with a care for significant detail worthy of one of the great Dutch painters, and the drawing of the physical structure of the old body enables one to visualise it as the fortress of an unconquerable spirit that had yielded to death, and in its upward sightlessness seemed trying to regain that spirit, to regain the guardianship it had just laid down.

Swithin took one look at the corpse and left the room. He could take nothing for dinner that evening but a partridge with an imperial pint of champagne. James of all the brothers and sisters manifested the most emotion. Tears rolled down the parallel furrows of his thin face. This would upset him for weeks! he thought resentfully. By this lack of control in the presence of death—for it is death itself rather than the loss of Ann, one feels, that works on his emotions —James reveals his own fear and the tenacity of his hold on life. And in this Galsworthy, prescient as all genuine creators of character are, foreshadows the terrible fight for life in which James engages when his time comes. His son, Soames, comes to him out of the black windy night. James's breathing was as if strangled; his eyes were closed. And in Soames, looking on his father so worn and white and wasted, listening to his strangled breathing, there rose a passionate vehemence of anger against Nature, cruel inexorable Nature, kneeling on the chest of that wisp of a body, slowly pressing out the breath, pressing out the life of the being who was dearest to him in the world. His father, of all men, had lived a careful life, moderate, abstemious, and this was his reward—

to have life slowly, painfully squeezed out of him! And without knowing that he spoke, he said: "It's cruel."

In this scene Soames is more emotional than ever before or after in the whole range of the Forsyte cycle, and his attractiveness is greatly enhanced. The most "sympathetic" thing he ever did was to tell the lie which made his father's death easier. Annette had borne him a daughter: he told James, who craved for male descent, that it was a son, and the old man made a queer noise, ugly, relieved, pitiful, triumphant—like the noise a baby makes getting what it wants. James's foot becomes uncovered. Soames takes it in his hand, a cold foot, light and thin, white, very cold, and warms it mechanically, listening to his father's laboured breathing. The minutes pass. Suddenly he started up; a sound, a dreadful sound such as he had never heard, was coming from his father's lips, as if an outraged heart had broken with a long moan . . . Dead! Later Soames came back and looked at the dead man, wonderfully calm, free from shadow and anxiety, with the gravity on his ravaged face which underlies great age, the worn fine gravity of old coins.

Violent sudden death is relatively rare in Galsworthy's work. Bosinney walks under a bus in a fog, intentionally, and is killed. We do not see the death, but again death serves as a focusing point for directing our gaze to the living. The four Forsytes looked at the sightless defiant face of the recalcitrant Bosinney in the mortuary, and in each one of them the secret emotions, fears, and pity of his own nature rose and fell like the rising, falling waves of life; and in each one of them the trend of his nature, the odd essential spring, which moved him in fashions

minutely, unalterably different from those of every
other human being, forced him to a different attitude
of thought. Soames gazes, white and still at this
dead man to whom his wife had yielded, and then
murmured and crept noiselessly away. Old James,
ever more demonstrative, hunted for a handkerchief
to wipe his brow; then, bending sorrowful and lank
over the dead man, he too turned and hurried out.
But Old Jolyon, himself old enough to be aware of the
relevance of death, stood long in meditation. Who
shall tell of what he was thinking? Of himself, when
his hair was brown like the hair of that young fellow
dead before him? Of himself, with his battle just
beginning, the long, long battle he had loved; the
battle that was over for this young man almost before
it had begun?—And Young Jolyon, who had the impersonal eye, walking sorrowfully away from the
hospital, reflected that this death would break up
the Forsyte family. The stroke had indeed slipped
past their defences into the very wood of their
tree.

Tryst, in *The Freelands*, having been sentenced to
three years' penal servitude for arson, attacked the
warders, threw himself under a motor-car and was
killed. Death's majesty had planed away the aspect
of brutality from his face, removed the yearning,
covering all with wistful acquiescence. Felix looked
on the frozen tranquillity of that body, meditating.
As the carved beauty of great buildings, so is the
graven beauty of death, the lonely wonder of the
abandoned thing lying so quiet, so far already from
what once lived!

The other violent deaths in Galsworthy usually
come as a logical climax to a sequence of events.
Dancy (*Loyalties*) finds the only way out of an im-

224

possible situation by firing a pistol neatly through the heart, leaving a note in which he says: "A pistol keeps faith." Stephen More (*The Mob*) is stabbed in a brawl. Not knowing that death was imminent, his last words were: "Don't think you can break my faith. You could never break or shake it, if you were a million to one." In his case the reward of death is a monument erected to his memory by his countrymen who, when he was alive, despised him. Falder (*Justice*), driven to despair, throws himself over the banisters and is killed--the only possible climax to a pursuit which would never have ended. The old clerk's last words have an unconscious cynicism which are irresistibly moving in the theatre: "No one'll touch him now! Never again! He's safe with gentle Jesus!" Clare, another *Fugitive*, also commits suicide, among strangers. "She was a lady. That's all I know about her," says the young man who had shown her kindness. Sudden and violent was the death which ended the second episode in *The Dark Flower*—the drowning at night of Mark Lennan's beloved. The incident is very graphically described. Lennan's awful struggle with roots and weeds and slime, a desperate agony of groping in that pitchy blackness, among tree-stumps, in dead water that seemed to have no bottom . . . a nightmare search more horrible than words could tell, till in a patch of moonlight on the bank they laid her, who for all their efforts never stirred. Whether the thoughts which derive from this incident are Lennan's or the author's own is not clear: Her spirit mingled now with the white beauty and the shadows, for ever part of the stillness and the passion of a summer night; hovering, floating, listening to the rustle of the reeds, and the whispering of the woods;

one with the endless dream—that spirit passing out, as all might wish to pass, in the hour of happiness.

Most beautiful is the passing of Old Jolyon. Beauty seemed to impregnate the closing months of his life, rounding it off and justifying it. He sits in the shade of a tree, waiting for Irene, smelling the scent of limes and lavender and listening to the excited buzzing of bees drugged on honey and happiness like himself. He closed his eyes, to take a nap, to be the more fresh when she should arrive. Some thistle-down came on what little air there was and pitched on his moustache more white than itself. He did not know; but his breathing stirred it. The dog Balthasar stretched and looked up at his master. The thistle-down no longer moved. The dog placed his chin over the sunlit foot. It did not stir. The dog withdrew his chin, quickly, rose, and leaped on Old Jolyon's lap, looked in his face, whined; then leaping down, sat on his haunches, gazing up. And suddenly he uttered a long long howl. But the thistle-down was still as death, and the face of his old master. Summer—summer—summer! The soundless footsteps on the grass.

Death came to the dog Balthasar from excess of joy at his master's return. Young Jolyon whistled and the obese old dog, a hundred yards away, got off his haunches and his tail, close-curled over his back, began a feeble, excited fluttering; he came waddling forward, gathered momentum, and disappeared over the edge of the fernery. When Jolyon turned into the fernery he saw the old dog looking up with eyes already glazing, with an expression in them that seemed to say: "I can't get up, master, but I'm glad to see you." He dies. The heart had simply failed

in the obese body from the emotion of his master's
return. Jolyon and his son Jolly bury the eighteen-
year-old dog. "Strange life a dog's," says Jolyon;
"the only four-footer with rudiments of altruism and
a sense of God!" And the occasion is improved by a
thoughtful dialogue on first principles which I have
quoted on another page.*

And before Jolyon himself passes into the darkness,
his face buried in the honey-suckle which he and
Irene had tended with such care, his son Jolly meets
a premature and solitary death in the Transvaal on
the verge of manhood; delirious, with consciousness
that ebbs and flows, agitated because his repeater-
watch does not strike . . . over the river—sleep!
He has gone. The waste of a life, for a cause of
which he was scarcely aware and in which he only
half-believed! It is as moving as the death of that
other boy, in Egypt, to whom the Reverend Edward
Pierson wished to minister comfort. Pierson waited
beside the unconscious boy, watching the sun sink.
If the boy might pass like this, he felt it would be
God's mercy. Then he saw the boy's eyes open,
wonderfully clear eyes of the lighted grey which had
dark rims. "I'm goin' West, zurr," the boy said.
Through Pierson's mind there flashed the thought:
"O God! Let me be some help to him!" "To God,
my dear son!" he said. And a flicker of humour, or
ironic question, passed over the boy's lips. . . . In
the boy's smile had been the whole of stoic doubt, of
stoic acquiescence. Later on, Pierson stands looking
at the afterglow. "The sun and the boy—together
they had gone West, into that wide glowing nothingness." Here again is an episode integral of the story,

* p. 216.

not dragged in to point a moral, but it etches in acid the tragedy of Pierson : the younger generation rejects him, smiling without faith, undaunted.

In the death of Soames are tied up all the loose threads of his life. Galsworthy, in general averse from symbolism, seems here to have released himself from the tyranny of his own realism, as on a few occasions he had done before. The man of property, who in early manhood had hoped to take beauty by force and love by purchase, at the end gives his life fighting with all his strength to save beauty from the ravages of fire, and receives his death-blow in protecting from harm the one creature whom he had unselfishly loved. This is not the place to follow the infinitely slow process by which the miraculous transformation takes place; that it does take place and leaves no residue of doubt to mar complete acceptance, has never, I think, been questioned. Three days pass before Soames "takes the ferry," three days of quiet struggle. Fleur watches him. The extraordinary tenacity of that struggle to come back terrified her. He *meant* to be a mind, he *meant* to know and hear and speak. It was as if he must die from the sheer effort of it. Father and daughter come together, in the fullest sense, for the first time. And suddenly, his eyes went out. There was nothing there ! (*Swan Song*.)

J. G. "TAKES THE FERRY" . . .

In November 1932 Galsworthy was to have joined me in Paris to attend an international committee meeting of the P.E.N. A day or two before I left London he had every intention of coming—and, characteristically, on 19th November, he wrote to me "Can you have sure definition of what 'tenue de ville (veston)' is by Monday?" lest he should not be

JOHN GALSWORTHY. VIENNA 1929.

To face p. 228.

rightly clad for the function in Paris which was designed primarily, no doubt, to do him honour. It was not until the day of the dinner that a telegram came announcing that he was not well enough to travel.

He had been looking unwell for some time, and there was an unaccustomed absence of vitality in his manner which ought to have warned me that all was not as it should be. But he made light of his indisposition, and it was not unusual for him to look extremely pale; indeed, except when burnt by the sun, his complexion was curiously colourless and added to that appearance of austerity which so belied him. It was round about this time that he was awarded the Nobel Prize and a number of members of the P.E.N. wished to show him, by some public function, how much they rejoiced in this recognition of his merits. The suggestion that a lunch or dinner should be given in his honour was dismissed by him with peculiar definiteness; he said, smiling, that if any such ceremony took place he would escape to the North Pole in good time to avoid it.

I saw him last on the 21st November at a committee of the P.E.N., when he told me—what indeed he had already written to me personally—that he intended to make over the Nobel Prize money to the London P.E.N. At this meeting he was very quiet, showing little of that whimsicality and quickness of mind which commonly enlivened such gatherings. The business of the committee disposed of, he stayed on, as if there were other matters to be dealt with, and the meeting came to an end from a sort of inanition rather than because the Chairman so decreed. After the rest of the members of the committee had gone, he still lingered and talked to me. His penultimate novel, *Flowering Wilderness*, which was dedicated to me, had recently appeared, and he told me how nobly the publishers had laboured to rectify a mistake in the spelling of my name. A few advance copies had gone out with "Herman" on the dedication page before the error had been noticed. One of these he had sent me, with the following letter on the flyleaf:—

"MY DEAR HERMON,

I hope this will be an unique possession for you, for not only is it an advance copy and probably the only one; but one in which your name is spelled wrong. I am stirring the waters under the earth to get the error corrected, but I shall be satisfied if I get the publishers above the earth to do the deed. You will, I hope, keep the foul affair to yourself.

Yours always,
JOHN GALSWORTHY."

Messrs. Heinemann, as soon as the mistake was discovered, set about correcting it; the printers worked night and day for forty-eight hours, and if my memory is not at fault, J.G. said that ninety thousand pages had to be scrapped and ninety thousand substituted for them, all on account of one wrong letter. His exasperation when my name was misspelled always seemed to me excessive: I have become so used to it!

I did not see him again. He said good-bye with that curiously beautiful smile which those who knew him will not forget. Several letters passed between us after this—most of them written by his wife and signed by him; and then the contact became no more than a series of inquiries by telephone. On 30th January I had a strangely vivid dream. Vivid, but inconsequent as dreams are. I was sitting with J.G. in what I knew to be his car but seemed, in some other part of my consciousness, to be a coach, drawn by two black horses. To be aware of the inside and the outside of the vehicle at the same time did not strike me as strange. Moreover, although I knew it was his car, I was not surprised that the upholstery was black, instead of grey. He was dressed in a long dark overcoat which was familiar to me, and he was muffled to the neck. His face was as pale as I had seen it last. In a curiously monotonous voice he talked about the committee of the P.E.N., as the coach swayed from side to side on a very irregular road, and through the windows I saw the pitch-black night. Presently the horses, with a curious padded pawing of the ground, stopped. A blurred figure opened the door and I rose to get out. I was surprised to find that J.G. did not move. I turned to him apprehensively, and asked him why he was not coming. "You get out here," he said, "but I go on." On hearing this I became intensely disturbed and pleaded with him to come with me; but he, faintly smiling, pressed my arm comfortingly, and told me to go. I alighted. The blurred figure which had opened the door, closed it behind me. Again that curious padding of the horses, and the black coach passed into the darkness, leaving me with a dreadful sense of desolation.

I confess that I was not surprised when I heard next morning that Galsworthy was dead.

"THE UNIMAGINABLE STATE"

The question of the soul's immortality, the persistence of personality after bodily death, was one which Galsworthy frequently touched on in his talks with me. His interest in it was sporadic but not shallow, and as it was never I who first raised the subject, it is possible that it was not often altogether remote from his mind. Throughout his works there are direct and indirect allusions to it and, although he never seems to have reached conviction one way or the other, it is not improbable that his interest grew as he grew older. Old Stone in *Fraternity*, who seems often to express views that may be legitimately attributed to Galsworthy, was peculiarly antagonistic to what he called that most irreligious fetish, the belief in the permanence of the individual ego after death, to the worship of which he attributed all the sorrows of the human race, including the insensate barbarism of taking human life. And many years later Gyp (*Beyond*) answers her father's question: "What do you think happens after death?" with "Nothing, Dad. I think we just go back"—not into the melting-pot, to be refashioned like buttons in the crucible of the Button-moulder, but back into the great sum of the universe, there to be absorbed, the personality snuffed out. "The religious Johnnies are saving their money to put on a horse that'll never run after all. Those Yogi chaps in India—there they used to sit, the world might rot for all they cared— they were going to be all right themselves, in Kingdom Come. But suppose it doesn't come."

The older Forsytes probably accepted the dogma of the immortality of the soul as they accepted any other institution which made for the stability of property, and in any case, as no expenditure was involved, they might as well be on the safe side; the next generation was more questioning and more guarded. Even Soames in his old age paused a moment in Winchester Cathedral and considered the predicted end of the world in 1928, deciding that if it did come to an end he, for one, would not mind. It had never been a great success, and if it were wiped out at one stroke there would be nothing left behind anyway: what was objectionable about death was leaving things that you were fond of behind. The moment, too, that the world came to an end, it would begin again, in some other shape, any way. (*Swan Song.*) And he listened to the choir boys singing: "He sendeth the springs into the rivers; which run among the hills. All the beasts of the fields drink thereof; and the wild asses quench their thirst . . . I will sing unto the Lord as long as I live; I will praise the Lord while I have my being . . . " and, lost among the shadows of the great cathedral, he probably approached as near to spirituality as his possessive soul would permit.

His successful rival, Young Jolyon, more prone to speculative thought, being not wholly Forsyte but half-artist, toyed with the idea of the persistence of the human spirit. In the room which had been his much-loved father's, he would catch a moment of communion, an atmospheric impact, like a scent, or one of those strong animistic impressions from forms, or effects of light, to which those with the artist's eyes are especially prone. His mind rebelled at the prospect of leaving his wife, his boy, his home, his work, for unknown darkness, for the unimaginable state, for such nothingness that he would not even be conscious of wind stirring leaves above his grave, nor of the scent of earth and grass. Such nothingness that, however hard he might try to conceive it, he never could, and must still hover on the hope that he might see again those he loved. To realise this was to endure very poignant spiritual anguish. But although wishes father thought, they don't breed evidence, and Young Jolyon could find nothing in support of the survival of personality which could not be explained by telepathy, subconsciousness, and emanations from the storehouse of this world. That this tallies with Galsworthy's own conclusions seems to be borne out by a couple of letters which he wrote a few years later to Mr. H. Dennis Bradley, with whose permission I quote the following extracts.

The first is dated 18th August 1923:

"I have been frightfully interested in that Daily News cutting. I always feel that those of us who are sceptical have to suppose a possible explanation almost if not fully as remarkable as the phenomenon of survival. In your case, for instance, it seems very far-fetched to advance as a possible explanation the idea that the medium was himself unconsciously mopping up from you (and perhaps other people not present) *sub*conscious knowledge of your sister, including physical characteristics, and reproducing it; while just adding, perhaps consciously, such remarks as 'Quite happy,' 'Always with you,' 'Wanting to speak with you,' which one seems to have heard often before. This power of mopping up all subconscious knowledge and having a sort of free access to the subconscious store of the world, and the power of reproducing it more or less coherently, may be—as it seems to me—the mediumistic gift, that, and that alone.

"On the other hand, as I say, this seems almost as 'super-natural' as the survival of spirits.

"You see, we have to admit that without the medium, nothing happens, and it does seem to me that this is in itself evidence of the mediumistic gift being responsible for the phenomena. The moment we get direct communication between spirit and a living person who clearly has not himself the mediumistic gift, we should have a much more convincing testimony to the possibility of survival.

"Knowing you, I should say yours was one of the most striking instances I ever read, but I don't think it disposes of that possible explanation."

From the second letter, dated 2nd October of the same year, I quote:

"You, certainly, have had experiences which must shake your faith. I don't know that I feel the 'intelligent' nature of the interviews to be much or any evidence. If the manifestations are the result of unknown subconscious powers—the mental equipment of those present would colour the tone of the communications; and I'm afraid you cannot plead guilty to lack of intelligence. I hope sincerely that you will get direct communication. I—like all, I suppose, who love or have loved deeply anyone in this life—wish the assurance that I will continue with them after death; but the very urgency of that longing makes one the more deeply distrustful—seeing how all life shows one the way that wishes father thoughts. Other than for that reason I don't think I want to travel on after the lamp here is broken up—there seems something stale and unnatural in the idea. Do keep me in touch however."

Seven years later, at Bury, the subject cropped up again. We were talking about a psychic experience of my own, intensely puzzling and inconclusive. (The curious will find a concise account of it in "Tales of Mystery" edited by Ernest Rhys and C. A. Dawson Scott.) The story was a long one, but J.G. insisted on my narrating it in detail and had clearly not abandoned his interest in the question of survival. He told me that he had had a sitting with one of the best-known mediums—Mrs. Osborn Leonard, I think it was—but had come away unconvinced and disinclined to follow up the matter. This was in the autumn of 1930. I do not recall that he ever alluded to the subject again in my presence. If he changed his mind, acquired conviction or faith, there is nothing in his later work that reveals it. To the delightful inconsequence of Aunt Em who seeks information on the hereafter, Dinny throws out the consoling thought that perhaps those who want one have it; but Adrian, the wise, states his belief unequivocally that spirits do not survive.

One thing is certain, Galsworthy would have found it difficult to believe in a doctrine which gave immortality to men and denied it to animals. The countryman in charge of the mare about to foal (*Buttercup Night*) had no doubts on the subject. "They zay 'orses 'aven't no souls. Many's the Christian ah've seen ain't got the soul of an 'orse;" and pressed for a further confession of faith, he adds: "For all they zay, ah don't think none of us goes such a brave way off. There's room for all, dead or alive. An' there's Christians ah've zeen—well, ef they'm not dead for gude, then neither aren't dumb animals, for sure." He admitted, however, that the whole question was "a bit dimsy-like."

"If *we* have spirits that persist," Galsworthy wrote in *Memories*, "*they* have. If *we* know after our departure who we were—*they* do." And the companion who shared in the allegiance of this beloved dog declared that she had seen him since his bodily death. He came to her in the visible shape of his black body, passing round the dining-table from the window-end, to his proper place beneath the table, at her feet. She saw him quite clearly; she heard the padding tap-tap of his paws and very toe-nails; she felt his warmth brushing hard against the front of her skirt. She thought then that he would settle down upon her feet, but something disturbed him, and he stood pausing, pressed against her, then moved toward where J. G. generally sat but was not sitting that night. She saw him stand there, as if considering; then at some sound or laugh, she became self-conscious, and slowly, very slowly, he was no longer there.

Hallucination? Who shall say?

The last allusion to such things is to be found in the letter from Adrian which closes *Over the River* and brings Galsworthy's work to an ill-timed end. He dwells on the impermanence of beauty—the lurking consciousness of mortality, perhaps knowledge that all things must slip away from one in time, and the greater their beauty the greater the loss in store!

Galsworthy thirsted after beauty as the saint after righteousness. He had no sympathy with the recent cult of ugliness in the plastic and graphic arts, nor with the glorification of cacophony in modern music; nor with the crudeness and rudeness of modern manners. The last poem in his collection of verse is a prayer *To Beauty*:

Bring me knowledge:
How the pansies are made, and the cuckoos'
song!
And the little owls, grey in the evening, three on
a gate;
The gold-cups a-field, the flight of the swallow;
The eyes of the cow who has calved;
The wind passing from ash-tree to ash-tree!

For thee shall I never cease aching?
Do the gnats ache that dance in the sun?
Do the flowers ache, or the bees rifling their
gold?
Is it I only who ache?
Beauty! Fulfil me! Cool the heart of my desire!

He was fully aware of the relativity of beauty as of
all things save some inscrutable Absolute which cannot be apprehended; but Beauty, however indefin-
able, yields at least temporary ecstasy to those who
seek her, even though she holds her pursuer at a distance and always eludes capture. I am sure that if
the grave and loving spirit of John Galsworthy still
persists in the universe, it walks the interstellar ways,
the candle of vision on its brow, pledged to a search
for Beauty for all eternity.

INDEX

INDEX

INDEX

England and Englishmen, 17–31, 80–81

Epstein's *Rima*, 75

Escape, 130, 140, 208

Evans, C. S., 74

Fairbridge, Dorothea, 83

Flowering Wilderness, The, 103, 159, 183–184, 208, 230

Flying, 108–109

Ford, Ford Madox, 122–123

Forest, The, 29, 127

Forsyte Saga, The (consult titles of the separate novels)

Forsytes, The, other references to, 23, 27–29, 36, 63, 67–68, 70, 152, 154, 160, 161, 190

Foundations, The, 50

France, Anatole, 20

Franck, César, 117

Fraternity, 22, 23, 26, 37, 82, 134, 155, 161, 163, 170, 191, 209, 232

Freelands, The, 24, 25, 58, 126, 134, 156, 179, 183, 213, 224

Fugitive, The, 128, 160, 225

Fuller, Edward, 64

Galsworthy, John, Death of, 228–231

Galsworthy, John, in War-time, 63–64

Galsworthy, Mrs., 63–64, 95, 118, 237

General Strike, 1926, 107–108

Greville, Ursula, 113

Hauptman, Gerhardt, 123

Hodgson, Ralph, 196

Horses, 195, 236

Humour, 139–145

Ibsen, 123

Immortality, 231–237

In Chancery, 43–44, 47, 65, 216, 227

Indian Summer of a Forsyte, 12, 111, 226

Inn of Tranquillity, The, 185, 194, 210

Island Pharisees, The, 19, 20, 30, 35, 114–115, 121, 143, 152, 155, 190, 207

Joy, 171, 199

Joyce, James, 103, 154

Justice, 38, 127, 140, 202, 225

Kennedy, Margaret, 104

Law, The, 36–39

Lawrence, D. H., 150–153

League of Nations, 73

Lewis, Sinclair, 20

Little Dream, The, 91

Little Man, The, 91, 140

Loyalties, 130, 133, 140, 224

MacCarthy, Desmond, 18, 19

242

INDEX